"For educational leaders who recognize that the most i
school happens in the classroom, this book provides p
how school leaders can support teaching and advance learning for every student. Written in a clear and accessible style, this book will be a tremendous resource for educators who seek to make a difference."

—*Pedro A. Noguera, PhD, distinguished professor of education, UCLA Graduate School of Education & Information Studies*

"Markholt, Michaelson, and Fink offer many insights into how administrators lead professional development while also surfacing numerous school conditions necessary to fuel and spread teaching practice. This important book also raises the possibility of collective leadership by principals and teachers for next generation school reforms that can better serve all students."

—*Barnett Berry, founder and CEO of the Center for Teaching Quality (CTQ)*

"This book is exactly what both aspiring and practicing instructional leaders need. Each chapter offers guidance on practical moves principals and teams can engage in that develop greater expertise through focused observation, targeted professional development, and support for refined teaching practice—all designed to improve student learning. The anchor case describes a school context that is realistic. The authors emphasize key points through the experiences of a principal and her leadership team and make the team's thinking visible."

—*Ann O'Doherty, EdD, associate dean, professional studies director, Danforth Educational Leadership Program; president, Washington Council for Educational Administration Programs, University of Washington, College of Education*

"When I began my years as a principal at a large urban high school in Pennsylvania, I remember how overwhelming the job was. At the same time, I also remember how much I craved practical, accessible books that I could read and apply what I gleaned immediately. I am happy to say that I found some of those books by authors like Phillip Schlecty, Anthony Bryk, Milbrey McGlauglin, and Beverly Danial Tatum. I wish this book by Markholt, Michaelson, and Fink was around during my time as a principal.

When it comes to school leadership, besides ensuring physical and emotional safety, I can't think of a more important responsibility of leaders than ensuring impactful professional learning for adults. Every principal, teacher leader, and instructional leadership team should read this book."

—*Irvin Scott, EdD, Harvard Graduate School of Education*

# Leading for Professional Learning

# Leading for Professional Learning

## What Successful Principals Do to Support Teaching Practice

Anneke Markholt
Joanna Michelson
Stephen Fink

Foreword by Stephanie Hirish

JB JOSSEY-BASS™

A Wiley Brand

Published by Jossey-Bass
A Wiley Brand
535 Mission Street, 14 FL; San Francisco CA 94105-3253—www.josseybass.com

Jossey-Bass books and products are available through most bookstores. To contact Jossey-Bass directly call our Customer Care Department within the U.S. at 800-956-7739, outside the U.S. at 317-572-3986, or fax 317-572-4002.

Wiley also publishes its books in a variety of electronic formats and by print-on-demand. Some material included with standard print versions of this book may not be included in e-books or in print-on-demand. If this book refers to media such as a CD or DVD that is not included in the version you purchased, you may download this material at http://booksupport.wiley.com. For more information about Wiley products, visit www.wiley.com.

**Library of Congress Cataloging-in-Publication Data**

Names: Markholt, Anneke, author. | Michelson, Joanna, author. | Fink, Stephen L., author.
Title: Leading for professional learning : what successful principals do to support teaching practice/Anneke Markholt, Joanna Michelson, Stephen Fink.
Description: San Francisco, CA : Jossey-Bass, 2018. | Includes bibliographical references and index.
Identifiers: LCCN 2018018044 (print) | LCCN 2018032091 (ebook) | ISBN 9781119440406 (Adobe PDF) | ISBN 9781119440437 (ePub) | ISBN 9781119440444 (pbk.)
Subjects: LCSH: Teachers—In-service training. | School administrators—In-service training. | Educational leadership.
Classification: LCC LB1731 (ebook) | LCC LB1731 .M2155 2018 (print) | DDC 370.71/1—dc23
LC record available at https://lccn.loc.gov/2018018044

Cover Design: Wiley
Cover Image: ©Tolga TEZCAN/Getty Images

Printed in the United States of America

FIRST EDITION

*PB Printing*   V10003831_090718

# CONTENTS

CONTENTS

# LIST OF FIGURES

# LIST OF TABLES

**Anneke Markholt, PhD,** is the associate director with the University of Washington Center for Educational Leadership (CEL) and affiliate associate professor at the University of Washington College of Education. Markholt designs and directs the center's partnerships focused on developing teaching effectiveness and instructional leadership. She is particularly interested in the intersection of teaching, learning, and the leadership capacity necessary for school systems to engage in instructional improvement, especially for linguistically diverse students. Prior to her work with CEL, Markholt spent five years as an associate researcher for the Center for the Study of Teaching and Policy at the University of Washington. She began her career as an English as a second language specialist for Tacoma Public Schools, where she taught for 10 years. Markholt is the coauthor of Leading for Instructional Improvement: How Successful Leaders Develop Teaching and Learning Expertise.

**Joanna Michelson, PhD,** is a project director at the University of Washington Center for Educational Leadership. She manages CEL's content area professional development and coach learning lines of services. She also provides direct support to teachers, coaches, and school and district leaders in secondary literacy instruction and coaching. Prior to full-time work at CEL, Joanna worked as a middle school language arts teacher, secondary literacy coach, and as a consultant for CEL. She completed her doctoral degree at the College of Education at the University of Washington with a focus on coach learning from practice.

**Stephen Fink, EdD,** is the former executive director of the University of Washington Center for Educational Leadership and affiliate professor of educational leadership and policy studies in the University of Washington College of Education. Fink has worked extensively with school and district leaders on improving the quality of instructional leadership. His work has spanned large urban, suburban, rural, and charter schools and management organizations across the country. In addition to directing CEL, Fink provides facilitation and executive coaching for superintendent and district-level leaders in a number of CEL partnerships. Prior to coming to the University of Washington he spent 12 years as an assistant superintendent in the Edmonds School District (WA) and was a principal and special education teacher in Idaho and Los Angeles. Fink is the coauthor of Leading for Instructional Improvement: How Successful Leaders Develop Teaching and Learning Expertise.

## ACKNOWLEDGMENTS

This book is the product of years of learning, collaborating, and exploring. As a service arm of the College of Education at the University of Washington, our thinking constantly grows and expands as we interact with dedicated and brilliant teachers and leaders across the country—and then we come back to CEL to engage in rich dialogue and reflection. Our work in the field is the heart of what we do, and we could not have produced this book without the willingness of our partners to open their practices and their worlds to us. As was the case in our first book, *Leading for Instructional Improvement* (2011), the tools, processes, and ideas are the result of our collective learning with our colleagues and our district partners. We remain grateful and honored for the opportunity to work to understand the complexities of real schools where our nation's teachers and children learn, take risks, and grow on daily basis.

All of our colleagues at CEL have contributed directly or indirectly to the concepts and strategies in this book. In the course of our work and collaboration as a team, we regularly share our experiences from the field, trying to figure out what our partners are learning, where they are succeeding, and where they are struggling. At CEL, we push each other to be better, and we know we are better as a result. We would not have the tools we have without our ongoing internal discourse. We thank each and every one of our project directors for their tireless work in the field, along with our outstanding office staff members who support their fabulous work back at home.

We would like to acknowledge specific contributions to the work described in this book. We thank Jennifer McDermott, whose creative ability to synthesize complex ideas led to the creation of the practical leadership tools that ground Chapters 4 through 6. She created the first iterations of these tools that now mediate countless leaders' abilities to collaboratively develop professional learning outcomes focused on students and teachers, engage in strategic professional learning planning, powerfully sponsor, and intentionally follow up on professional learning. We would also like to acknowledge Max Silverman, the primary architect of CEL's central office transformation work, including the development and design of the Principal Support Framework. We also thank Max for his thoughtful reading of and feedback on several chapters in this book.

We are constantly humbled by the brilliance and grace of our math and literacy consultants, who seamlessly shift their attention from students to teachers to leaders. Our consultants embody their beliefs that all students deserve the chance to think, argue, and *breathe* as mathematicians, readers, and writers and that with appropriate collaboration and instructional strategies, our teachers can get them there.

Although the case used in this book is partially fictionalized and we use pseudonyms, it is based on an actual middle school. Each time we sit down to write or revise the ideas in this book, we are inspired and motivated by the incredible energy, passion, and commitment of the teachers and leaders at this school. They are the ones we picture as we consider how to frame our narrative and our analysis. We have been honored to watch the school develop and grow across the years, learning from their own ups and downs, keeping their eyes on the success of their most vulnerable students. We have learned alongside its humble leaders, who wake up with the dedication required to do the practical work of creating a community of adult learners who strive continuously to improve the quality of learning for their students. To these teachers and leaders, we say a tremendous thank you!

I am always struck by those who wrestle with the concept of what it means to teach so others learn, such as Brian Dassler, the former deputy chancellor for the Florida Department of Education, who passed away recently at too young an age. Brian always spoke passionately about the fact that many don't appreciate or understand the complexity of teaching. He believed that if stakeholders understood what it means to teach so that all students learn, they wouldn't be looking for silver bullets to fix schools or blaming teachers for the problems in schools. Rather, they would recognize the importance of investing time and resources in educator learning—the high-leverage pathway to improving what happens in schools.

I had the privilege of working with Brian alongside Stephen Fink through a recent collaborative effort, and clearly Stephen and his coauthors of this new book, Anneke Markholt and Joanna Michelson, embrace the notion that teaching done well is at the heart of school improvement. In their earlier work, *Leading for Instructional Improvement* (2011), Fink and Markholt elevated the concept of expertise in learning as well as teaching and how to support it. In this book, Markholt, Michelson, and Fink translate their lessons learned into powerful tools and processes that will advance a vision consistent with ours at Learning Forward—excellent teaching and learning every day. The authors start from the premise that developing teaching expertise in principals is essential to effective school leadership and then outline strategies to do so.

At Learning Forward, we posit that the essential pathway to achieving improved practice is through the Standards for Professional Learning. These seven standards define the critical elements of professional learning essential to improving knowledge, skills, and practice that lead to improved outcomes for students. The standards apply to all educator learning, whether for a central office administrator, principal, or classroom teacher.

I'm always excited to see resources that help educators bring the Standards for Professional Learning to life in schools. Among the seven standards is one on leadership:

Professional learning that increases educator effectiveness and results for all students requires skillful leaders who develop capacity, advocate, and create support systems for professional learning.

As the explanation for the standard states, "Leaders throughout the pre-K–12 education community recognize effective professional learning as a key strategy for supporting significant school and school system improvements to increase results for all" (Learning Forward, p. 28).

Essential tools and processes for transferring the leadership standard into practice can be found throughout the chapters of *Leading for Professional Learning*. The authors offer guidance for the essential actions for leaders to take to develop their own expertise even as they create learning structures so teachers learn as well. The authors have worked alongside leaders helping them transform their schools into cultures that elevate learning and appreciate the complexity of teaching. They are not espousing what must be done; they are showing readers how to get it done.

The leadership standard calls on leaders to prioritize three actions, and I'm thrilled to see all three emphasized in this essential new work. The first is to *build capacity for learning and leading in others:* "Leaders recognize that universal high expectations for all students require ambitious improvements in curriculum, instruction, assessment, leadership practices, and support systems. These improvements require effective professional learning to expand educators' knowledge, skills, practices, and dispositions" (Learning Forward, p. 28).

Through the lens of a middle school case study and the University of Washington Center for Educational Leadership's 4 Dimensions of Instructional Leadership, Markholt, Michelson, and Fink present numerous opportunities for learning and reflection on the role of leaders in achieving the vision. In particular, the tool in Chapter 4 highlights the thinking behind the design of learning opportunities, making an explicit decision based on the outcomes one is seeking. Chapter 6 brings improvement full circle by focusing on tools that strengthen feedback to support implementation of new learning. Early chapters also address valuable tools for guiding observations of classroom practice, a process that the authors hold is not solely the responsibility of the principal but must be practiced by many if excellent teaching is to spread throughout a school.

Second, the leadership standard calls on leaders to *be advocates for professional learning:* "Leaders clearly articulate the critical link between increased student learning and educator professional learning. As advocates for professional learning, leaders make their own career-long learning visible to others. . . . Their actions model attitudes and behavior they expect of all educators" (Learning Forward, p. 29).

In the first chapter, Markholt, Michelson, and Fink make the case for leaders' explicit role in teacher learning and leaders' responsibility to further their own expertise in teaching. It is much more important that leaders walk the walk than talk the talk.

Chapter 5 offers a tool that helps leaders consider their role as learners and leaders in teachers' professional development. In particular, principals understand how their role is more than just offering learning opportunities and sitting in to demonstrate support for others' learning. Although our field overall is recognizing that instructional leadership is core to successful principalship, this book's emphasis on leaders developing deep teaching expertise breaks new, critical ground.

The leadership standard's third essential responsibility is *creating support systems and structures:* "Skillful leaders establish organizational systems and structures that support effective professional learning and ongoing continuous improvement. They equitably distribute resources to accomplish individual, team, and school goals" (Learning Forward, p. 30). *Leading for Professional Learning* includes a chapter on the support systems necessary for the kind of principal learning the authors outline. A district's learning system has the responsibility to develop teaching and learning expertise at all levels so that leaders can offer teachers the feedback and ongoing support required for all students to experience effective teaching each day.

I'm grateful that through this book Markholt, Michelson, and Fink present pragmatic tools and a framework essential for improving teaching and learning from the principal's perspective. They have put a laser focus on quality teaching and highlight the key elements essential to it. They also remind us of the importance of school leaders in ensuring that all students have access to quality teaching. This book will inspire those who serve as school leaders and those who aspire to lead.

Stephanie Hirsh, PhD, Learning Forward

## REFERENCE

Learning Forward. (2011). *Standards for professional learning.* Oxford, OH: Author.

Our nation has work to do. Deep and historically entrenched economic, political, and social chasms continue to create systemic barriers to student learning that result in educational disparities, dividing our nation's children along the lines of race, class, and language. Our efforts to improve educational outcomes for each and every student is multifaceted and remains the equity and social justice issue of our time.

At the Center for Educational Leadership (CEL), we continue to note that low expectations for some students often become a self-fulling prophecy: educators reinforce their own beliefs about students based on what they see in student engagement and classroom performance. When educators report that students "cannot do it," they are right, which reinforces a belief of low expectations. And the reason educators are "right" when they report that students "cannot do it," is that educators have yet to develop the depth of expertise necessary to overcome systemic barriers to student learning. Educators' expertise can impact their own attitudes and beliefs about students' capacity to learn. When educators can see, with their own eyes, the difference that their teaching practices make for their students' abilities to engage and succeed, expectations and perceptions of ability change. Developing teaching and learning expertise so that it affects practice and beliefs is an enormous, complex challenge and one that is vastly underestimated. In this book, we tackle just one aspect of this complex challenge.

This book is for leaders who want to create a culture for learning and design optimum learning experiences for themselves and the teachers in their schools. It is our belief that the ongoing work of improving the quality of teaching and learning is complex and requires school leaders to consider this complexity as they plan to support teachers' learning. This book brings forward practical ideas we designed for school leaders and their leadership teams—tools and processes to help leaders identify, in a much more fine-grained way, how to create cultures of adult learning and improved performance that lead ultimately to changes in the learning experiences teachers create for students.

## WHAT WE'RE LEARNING

Since our previous book, *Leading for Instructional Improvement* (Fink & Markholt, 2011), we continue to learn about the role of expertise and how school leaders can develop their own and others' expertise. We noted the lack of attention to expertise in educational policy and leadership literature and argued that if expertise influences what and how we see in any domain—for instance, in a garden, on a baseball field when a game is in progress, or on a chessboard—it follows that leaders' expertise about high-quality instruction will influence what they notice in a classroom and how they imagine what needs to improve. In our first book, we noted there are two kinds of expertise and that expertise begets expertise. *Learning* expertise "involves the degree to which would-be experts continually attempt to refine their skills and attitudes towards learning—skills and attitudes that include practicing, self-monitoring, and finding ways to avoid plateaus and move to the next level" (Bransford & Schwartz, 2008, p. 3) and *teaching* expertise—which is the difference between knowing math and knowing how to teach math. Six years later, we are still exploring these questions of leaders' expertise, helping them develop ample understanding of the sophisticated work of teaching as they learn alongside teachers about what is possible for students to achieve and how teachers create powerful learning experiences.

Also since our last book, shifts in teacher evaluation policy have taken center stage for many school leaders as they learn new evaluation frameworks and seek to become "reliable" raters of teaching practice. Yet despite the focus on reliable teacher evaluation practices, our experience in school districts across the country tells us that we still do not have a fully developed or shared vision for describing ambitious teaching and learning, let alone the expertise to realize this vision for each and every student. In order to improve the quality of teaching and learning, school leaders not only need a clear vision of what "high quality" looks and sounds like but also they need to know how to go about an improvement effort.

Further, as Tony Bryk and colleagues (2015) assert, teacher evaluation data can signal *where* improvements are needed, but this data rarely provide the kind of detail that teachers and schools need for *how* to improve. As they note, our ambitions for student learning continue to rise, but our collective know-how to realize these ambitions has not kept pace. We simply have not figured out how to teach each and every student to these higher standards. Our vision of what we mean by high-quality instruction and student engagement in rigorous learning experiences has continued to evolve, but there is still a wide chasm between our growing aspirations for all students and what we actually know how to do.

Although we considered the idea of "expertise" in our last book, we continue to learn from this body of research (Ericsson & Pool, 2016), and over the years we have worked with leaders to develop the kind of conditions at their schools that will promote learning for adults. As a profession, we have expectations and training for what teachers need to learn, but in our experience, schools tend to lack the conditions necessary for teachers to hone increasingly sophisticated practices, let alone conditions for school leaders that enable them to learn and lead alongside teachers. To get better at anything, we need to have access to more expert others as well as the time and place for the deliberate practice of skills that become more complex over time. This means that we need to be able to take risks with our practice and get feedback and coaching. We have helped leaders recognize and remove the barriers that get in the way of creating a culture for learning and that enable adults to shift habits and ways of thinking and *doing*, not only for teachers' practice but also for their own.

## PRACTICAL CONTENTS

In this book school and district leaders will find practical tools and processes that will help to develop a shared vision for improving the quality of student learning and teaching practice, interrupt a school culture of autonomous and private classroom practice, cultivate shared ownership for an improvement process, help create a school culture where expertise can be nurtured by norms of feedback and deliberate practice and that help school district leadership consider how to create system-wide conditions that support principal instructional leadership. We illustrate these ideas using a partially fictionalized case, based on a middle school and its school leader we have supported over the years. All names are pseudonyms.

**Chapter 1, "Focusing Teacher Learning,"** makes the case for leaders' explicit role in teacher learning and how leaders are pressed to develop further expertise in teaching, learning, and their reciprocal accountability for teachers' learning. The reader is introduced to a middle school and its principal to help illuminate the tools and processes featured throughout the ensuing chapters.

**Chapter 2, "Toward a Broader Definition of Instructional Leadership,"** situates the work of the instructional leader inside the University of Washington Center for Educational Leadership's (CEL) framework, the 4 Dimensions of Instructional Leadership™. We will use the case of the middle school principal to illustrate the 4D concepts and to identify the thread of ideas within the 4D for supporting teacher learning. We will build on the case of this middle school context, its students, teachers, and the state of teaching and learning the principal set out to improve in a living example of *reciprocal accountability,* which is one of CEL's core foundational ideas.

**Chapter 3, "The Role of Observation in Supporting Teachers' Learning,"** takes the reader into the middle school where the leadership team is preparing to observe in classrooms. This chapter explores the complexity of classroom observations, using CEL's 5 Dimensions of Teaching and Learning™ to illustrate how this framework can help to cultivate expertise for what we see in classrooms. Chapter 3 also highlights tools and processes that help leaders develop the discipline for a strength-based stance, that is, the discipline of formatively assessing teaching and learning in a way that supports leaders to see potential and to build from there versus taking a deficit-based approach to gathering observational data for the purposes of improvement.

**Chapter 4, "Planning for Focused Professional Learning,"** is an explanation of a key tool and process that our middle school case example will illustrate. The tool in this chapter brings forward the habit of thinking behind the design of teacher learning opportunities, making explicit connections among teachers' professional development (PD) sessions, formative classroom observations, and the strategic use of resources to generate optimum conditions for teachers' learning over time, leveraging the capacity that has been built.

**Chapter 5, "Sponsoring Professional Learning,"** brings forward another tool that helps leaders sharpen their articulation of the rationale for teacher learning and helps leaders consider the nature of their role as learners and leaders in teachers' PD. This tool helps to develop a discipline for articulating the why behind what we do and helps leaders consider the explicit link between what their behavior can model and how their sponsorship of teachers' learning is more than sitting in with them during PD.

**Chapter 6, "A Process for Following Up,"** explores the final tools and processes we will illustrate in this book. In this chapter, we provide explicit guidance for creating targeted feedback cycles linked to teachers' learning. We will illustrate a disciplined process to create feedback cycles that support teachers' implementation of new learning and that help leaders leverage these cycles as direct support for teachers and formative assessment opportunities for subsequent PD planning. This chapter also contains specific suggestions for how to make the most of a consultant's expertise, maximizing the time the consultant is with teachers and leveraging the consultant's expertise for the school's work in-between the consultant's visits.

In **Chapter 7, "A Call for System Action to Support Principals as Instructional Leaders,"** we zoom out from the middle school context to consider the role of the district office and illustrate how the principal in our case is able to work in the way described in the preceding chapters. We will introduce the reader to the ideas from

CEL's Principal Support Framework and discuss the reciprocal through line from the principal to the district, illustrating what support for the principal in this case looks like. This chapter will put the book in a broader systems perspective, asking the reader to consider the complex nature of improving teaching and learning, the principal's role, and the implications for the quality of support that principals need in order to improve the quality of teaching and learning.

In **Chapter 8, "Conclusion,"** we ask the reader to consider again the complexity of creating the conditions for adult learning that will lead to the development of expertise and a culture of improvement that result in student learning.

## REFERENCES

Bransford, J., & Schwartz, D. S. (2008). It takes expertise to make expertise: Some thoughts about why and how and reflections on the themes in chapters 15–18. In K. A. Ericsson (Ed.), *Development of professional expertise: Toward measurement of expert performance and design of optimal learning environments.* New York, NY: Cambridge University Press.

Bryk, A., Gomez, L., Grunow, A., & LeMahieu, P. (2015). *Learning to improve: How America's schools can get better at getting better.* Cambridge, MA: Harvard Education Press.

Ericsson, K. A., & Pool, R. (2016). *Peak: Secrets from the new science of expertise.* New York, NY: Houghton Mifflin Harcourt.

Fink, S., & Markholt, A. (2011). *Leading for instructional improvement: How successful leaders develop teaching and learning expertise.* San Francisco, CA: Jossey-Bass.

# Leading for Professional Learning

# Focusing Teacher Learning

Rachel Moriarty is the founding principal at Mountain View Middle School. She opened the school four years ago with the support of a brand-new assistant principal and a largely novice teaching staff. The school has grown year-by-year, reaching 925 students this fall, with an increasingly diverse student population in a neighborhood that used to be predominantly white and middle class. Now, although a third of the school has been designated "highly capable" (a group that tested into this program in first grade and also tends to be largely white and upper middle class), more than half of the population receives a free and reduced price lunch—including a growing homeless population.

As a whole, a little more than half the student population is white, 14% are Asian, 10% Latino, and 8% African American. There is a growing population of students who are also English language learners (ELLs), with more than 40 languages spoken at the school. The majority of the ELLs come from Spanish-speaking families, mainly from Central America. There is also an East African population, mostly Somali, in addition to some Eritrean and Ethiopian students. The ELL population is diverse in terms of schooling background. Some have attended public schools their whole lives and some had interrupted schooling prior to immigrating. Students' math test scores have shown a wide discrepancy between students of color, particularly the ELL students, and white students. Rachel, the principal, has noted over the past few years that Mountain View Middle School at times seems more like two schools—the "honors" and the "regular" school.

The challenge for Rachel is typical for school leaders who strive to foster rigorous and relevant learning experiences for each student at their schools. School leaders who are not satisfied with an existing status quo that tends to sort students along lines of race, class, and language face an enormous task—one that starts from the assumption that all students can learn, that learning depends on teachers creating powerful learning opportunities for their students, and that creating these learning opportunities for students is an incredibly complex and sophisticated endeavor. Not only do school leaders have to consider how to confront the implicit bias toward students of color or in poverty but also how to help teachers make shifts in their practice that will ask more of their students and that can challenge current conceptions of what students are capable of.

Rachel saw the gap in her students' math performance levels and knew something needed to change instructionally, but she was unsure about what those changes would be. Though she had taught for a decade, her own content expertise was in language arts, and she knew she needed to learn more about the shifts in math standards, how students learn these new content demands, and how teachers come to learn to these shifts. Rachel knew that the math teachers, by and large, knew their content area well and had a sense of what students should be able to do in sixth-, seventh-, and eighth-grade mathematics. However, she knew that the teachers did not know how to create enough scaffolding for students to be able to access the content that was presented. Furthermore, the more experienced teachers were also largely satisfied with what they were doing in the classroom. Given her own instructional background, Rachel could not yet name the specific changes in math instruction she wanted to see or what the teachers needed to learn to get there. But her own prior experience taught her that seeing what students are capable of, as a result of powerful teaching and learning opportunities, helps shift perceptions and expectations of what students can do. Indeed, John Hattie's research underscores this point: teachers' beliefs about their students' ability to learn and teachers' sense of efficacy about their impact on student learning is related to expertise. Expert teachers believe and expect their students to rise to the degree of challenge they present and they attend to the nature and the quality of the effect that they are having on every student (Hattie, 2009).

## THE PRINCIPAL'S CHALLENGE

Instructional leaders face considerable challenges requiring instructional leadership expertise. They must figure out what teachers need to learn as well as how to orchestrate and nurture teacher learning that results in the improvement of teaching practices. In 2003, Stein and Nelson proposed that school leaders' understanding of a content area (e.g., mathematics), how it is learned, and how it is taught are critical components of instructional leadership. As they considered this challenge for leaders, Stein and Nelson proposed the idea of "post holing," or leaders' ability to draw from their expertise in one content area in order to understand how to support teacher learning in another content area. Thus, they argued, instructional leadership skills may be transferrable between content areas.

For Rachel, the newly state-mandated teacher evaluation system helped her move past binary ideas of "satisfactory" or "unsatisfactory" teaching to rubrics with more descriptions to help gauge the quality of teaching. Yet replacing the "sat/un-sat" ratings with a four-point rubric does not fully define what a 4 looks and sounds like for particular grade levels and content areas, as well as what it takes to develop teachers' practice toward that definition. This level of expertise requires more than "rater reliability" training. As well, the higher standards put in place over the last six years (e.g., Common Core, Next Generation Science Standards) have helped shape ideas of the level of rigor and student engagement we hope to see, but closing the gap between what we can envision for our students and what teachers know how to do will require even more support from leaders. Putting student learning standards and an evaluation tool in leaders' hands is not enough to help nurture and support the development of teachers' practice. Additionally, as the efficacy of professional learning opportunities typically offered to teachers has come into question (Bill & Melinda Gates Foundation, 2014; The New Teacher Project, 2015), principals' roles in supporting teacher learning, versus compliance exercises, requires leaders to consider *how* they invest their leadership efforts to create and sustain relevant learning opportunities for teachers.

Because Rachel could draw on her expertise in language arts and experience supporting teachers' learning in literacy, she knew that the math department needed the kind of learning opportunities that cultivated changes in beliefs about what students were capable of and the development of instructional practices that helped teachers see the link between their specific teaching and what students could do as result. She knew that she would also have to support teachers' capacity to collaborate on and collectively problem-solve the instructional problems of practice that would emerge as teachers tried out new ways to scaffold student learning. She knew she had to support habits of collaboration and problem-solving in her math team: there were two veteran teachers with more than 10 years' experience among the group of largely novices, and she wanted to capitalize on their leadership potential as well as develop the entire team's capacity to learn with and from one another.

## THE CHALLENGE OF PROFESSIONAL LEARNING

There is a high bar for learning opportunities for teachers: learning opportunities are effective insofar as we can see the impact on the quality of classroom learning experiences for students. Although indeed a high bar for teacher learning, as we've learned from the research on "expertise," becoming more expert in anything (in this case, teaching) is about the *doing*—the actual performance. And although there are standards for professional learning and wide agreement for what constitutes "quality" professional development (Learning Forward, 2011), as a field we often miss the mark when it comes to creating ongoing learning opportunities that increase teachers' expertise over time and that result in improved student learning. For leaders, creating a culture of continuous improvement and a collective effort to solve problems of student learning is as complex as teaching itself.

Katz and Dack (2013) assert that professional learning for teachers often lacks clear focus, collaborative inquiry that will challenge thinking and current practice, and formal and informal instructional leadership. Their research underscores (1) the importance of "intentional interruptions" that help teachers question current understandings and practice and (2) the role of instructional leadership to support teachers' learning and hold teachers accountable for their learning. In the following chapter, and using the case of our middle school leader, we will explicate what we mean by *instructional leadership* as it is described in our 4 Dimensions of Instructional Leadership framework and will say more about how leaders support teachers' learning and hold teachers accountable.

When we consider what it takes to develop expertise—that is, the ongoing opportunity for deliberate practice with feedback and coaching (Ericsson & Pool, 2016)—and we pause to consider the enormous complexity of teaching, the findings from The New Teacher Project's Mirage study (2015) should not be a surprise. This study highlights the need for a definition of "development" toward an ambitious standard of teaching and student learning, with clear, deep understanding of performance and process. The Mirage study asserts that teachers' skills plateau, seldom reaching the skill level that will help engage their students in the kind of critical thinking that leads to students' conceptual understanding or to active ownership of their own learning, especially as it relates to the teaching and learning shifts described in the Common Core and Next Generation Science Standards:

> Like a mirage, [helping teachers improve] is not a hallucination but a refraction of reality: Growth is possible, but our goal of widespread teaching excellence is further out of reach than it seems. . . Much of this work involves creating the conditions that foster growth, not finding quick-fix professional development solutions. (The New Teacher Project, 2015, p. 3)

The fact is, we will continue to underestimate the conditions needed to foster the improvement of teaching practice until we come face-to-face with what it takes to develop expertise. Ericsson and Pool (2016, p. 204) write that *learning* means you are developing "mental representations," increasingly sophisticated mental maps of concepts, how those concepts connect, and how to analyze them, which enables you to figure out what needs improving and then come up with ways to realize that improvement. We do not develop increasingly detailed mental representations by sheer experience; rather, we need an expert alongside us to help us "see" and to engage in deliberate practice of a skill set, taking risks to push ourselves out of the comfort zone of what we already know how to do, to purposeful practice of a new skill over time. If we apply what we know about "job-embedded" professional development to the actual work of teachers, with the idea of developing increasingly sophisticated mental representations of, for example, what it looks and sounds like to engage and formatively assess a group of nine-year-olds as they navigate a narrative nonfiction chapter book for the first time, then we can begin to think through the kind of deliberate practice that will be necessary to develop such complex practices. Engaging in deliberate practice requires us to address the norms of privacy and autonomy that tend to keep teachers from working and learning with and from one another. Figuring out how to focus on teacher performance and how to improve it has, in this case, nothing to do with new teacher evaluation policy; rather, it has everything to do with getting better (Ericsson and Pool, 2016):

> When you look at how people are trained in the professional and business world, you find a tendency to focus on knowledge at the expense of skills. The main reasons are tradition and convenience: it is much easier to present knowledge to a large group of people than it is to set up the conditions under which individuals can develop skills through practice (p. 131). . . . what is ultimately most important is what people are able to do; training should focus on doing rather than on knowing (p. 138). . . . You pick up the necessary knowledge in order to develop the skills. (p. 250)

In other words, helping teachers to unpack standards and plan for lessons requires bringing skills into focus, not just knowledge (*knowing* what a standard says and *doing* something with that knowledge, in this case, creating a lesson plan). However, this kind of learning opportunity will not help teachers practice the specific skills required to enact a complex, standards-based lesson, paying attention to each student and formatively assessing student understanding as teaching is in progress. If we want teachers to "learn" standards, we should ask ourselves what teachers would *do* as the result of this learning. What change in behavior would we expect from a particular learning opportunity? We posit that teachers need ongoing opportunities that get right into *practice*, approximating and getting feedback and coaching along the way. Creating a lesson plan is one thing. Enacting the plan, responding to student thinking as they engage in the tasks, and capturing relevant information from the students to inform subsequent planning, for individual students, groups, and the entire class, is a series of complex skill sets that ultimately get at the practice of teaching toward standards.

Stein and Nelson's (2003) idea of post holing is akin to Ericsson's research on the development of skills and mental representations; that is, mental representations developed in one area can help us understand not only what it takes to be successful in that area but also enables us to apply that learning to other areas. We learn what "high-quality practice" entails and we can replicate it.

Drawing from her own understanding of high-quality language arts practice, principal Rachel set out to build the capacity of the Mountain View Middle School math department. In the second year of the school's existence, Rachel hired a math consultant (Andrea Jones), who met with the department and facilitated department discussion and classroom-based professional learning focused on discourse in math classrooms. Across the year, the team learned about the complexity of what it took to create classrooms where students could own and use mathematical academic language to describe their thinking and reasoning. Prior to this professional learning, teachers had not planned for student talk in math and did not collaborate with their colleagues to plan lessons or discuss what it meant to "engage" students. Typically, only a handful of students would talk and mostly to answer the teacher rather than each other. The department is now aiming for spaces where students can teach each other and teachers are now collaborating in service of students' success. The teachers find the professional learning relevant and helpful.

However, although Rachel sees some change in her two most experienced teachers' rooms and can hear differences in how teachers are talking with each other about their planning, she cannot tell if the majority of the classrooms are changing very quickly. Furthermore, the math scores are largely the same in year two as they were in year one of the school.

Leaders have an explicit role to play as they envision and enact professional learning for teachers, yet we do not see this as a hierarchical or "the expert" stance. Rather, in our view the leaders' role is about reciprocal accountability—we believe that holding teachers "accountable" for specific expectations for classroom practice means that leaders have an abiding responsibility to support teachers' learning. We are not suggesting a threshold amount for what is "enough" content knowledge that leaders need in order to understand how to learn and teach a subject area, thereby using this understanding to support teachers' learning. But the more leaders know about how students come to learn, for instance, seventh-grade mathematics, and the discipline-specific practices teachers can employ to help them learn, the more they will be able to see in a seventh-grade math classroom. Although novice mathematics observers may notice general instructional practices, such as whether or not teachers ask students to talk to partners and if students stay on task when asked to do so, more expert observers may notice the scaffolding and level of rigor in the specific tasks teachers provide students that prompt the partner talk. Experts may take a moment to compare the level of student thinking to the standards for the grade level and topic under study. These observers may also notice the language students use to express and justify their thinking as well as how students press each other for explanations and generalizations. Expertise influences leaders' abilities to notice, pose questions, and hypothesize about what they are seeing and will influence what they consider to be in need of improvement for teachers' practice. And, the more leaders can "see," the more specific their feedback and more targeted their professional learning design will be.

We are making the case for leaders to always consider the challenges and complexity of what it takes for teachers to make shifts in their practice. This includes the demands of content knowledge, but just as important, helping teachers learn requires leaders to create the conditions for teachers' learning. If a school's culture makes it difficult for teachers to take risks with their practice and receive feedback and coaching, then school leaders have to be strategic about how to interrupt this norm of isolation. At the end of the day, to learn a new skill, we need ample opportunities for practice with feedback. In school settings, the conditions necessary for teacher learning are in short supply and leaders have a role to play in setting the conditions. Education researchers have long noted that teaching is traditionally a private, closed-door endeavor with deference to seniority over expertise (Johnson & Donaldson, 2007; Lortie, 1975). Recognizing and addressing the barriers to teacher learning, creating ways of working with and among teachers, is the essence of reciprocal accountability. In subsequent chapters, we present tools and processes that illustrate habits of mind to help leaders enact their role of reciprocal accountability, from how to work from teachers' strengths to how to initiate and sustain a co-inquiry stance for improvement.

## DISCUSSION QUESTIONS

1. What professional learning challenges do you face in your school?

2. What barriers to collaboration and public practice might you need to address?

3. How would you describe the current state of instructional practice? What instructional practice expertise needs to be developed?

## REFERENCES

Bill & Melinda Gates Foundation. (2014). *Teachers know best: Teachers' views on professional development*. Seattle, WA: Author.

Ericsson, K. A., & Pool, R. (2016). *Peak: Secrets from the new science of expertise*. New York, NY: Houghton Mifflin Harcourt.

Hattie, J. (2009). *Visible learning: A synthesis of over 800 meta-analyses relating to achievement*. London, UK: Routledge.

Johnson, S., & Donaldson, M. (2007). Overcoming the obstacles to teacher leadership. *Educational Leadership, 65*(1), 8–13.

Katz, S., & Dack, L. (2013). *Intentional interruptions: Breaking down learning barriers to transform professional practice*. Thousand Oaks, CA: Corwin.

Learning Forward. (2011). *Standards for professional learning*. Oxford, OH: Author.

Lortie, D. (1975). *Schoolteacher: A sociological study*. Chicago, IL: University of Chicago Press.

The New Teacher Project. (2015). *The mirage: Confronting the hard truth about our quest for teacher development*. Brooklyn, NY: Author.

Stein, M. K., & Nelson, B. (2003). Leadership content knowledge. *Educational Evaluation and Policy Analysis, 25*(4), 423–448.

# Toward a Broader Definition of Instructional Leadership

Instructional leadership is a type of leadership aimed at improving the quality of learning for each student. It begins with a compelling vision, codeveloped and shared by the entire school community, coupled with strategic action that galvanizes teachers and staff members to learn about and improve their practice on behalf of student learning. A shared vision implies that teachers, collectively, attend to the nature and the quality of the effect that they are having on each student, supporting one another to create the optimal classroom environment for learning. As an instructional leader, a principal must cultivate a collective enterprise of improvement as well as constantly till the soil to nurture the development of the school's capacity to engage in continuous improvement. A principal must marshal and deploy resources strategically as well as manage people and processes in ways that further the vision of a learning-focused culture.

As noted previously, Rachel, the principal, faced a daunting challenge when she opened Mountain View Middle School. Given all the competing demands for a principal's energy and focus, how did Rachel figure out where to put her time and effort on a daily basis? Among all the possible leadership actions that Rachel could take, which ones would be more likely to make the biggest difference in improving teaching and learning? Given the school context, what should Rachel do first? In this chapter, we introduce the reader to the 4 Dimensions (4D) of Instructional Leadership framework and situate Rachel's decision-making therein, examining the 4D framework along-side the leadership actions Rachel undertakes as she sets out to improve the quality of teaching and learning at Mountain View Middle School. We highlight the 4D as a lens into the complexity of instructional leadership, inviting the reader to think about each dimension as its own lens as well as how the four dimensions interrelate.

## THE 4 DIMENSIONS OF INSTRUCTIONAL LEADERSHIP

Research shows that principals spend an average of only 8–17% of their time (Jerald, 2012), or three to five hours per week (Supovitz & May, 2011), in instructional leadership activities. And this same research suggests that some of the work principals are doing in instructional leadership lacks the focus needed to improve instruction. Therein lies much of the challenge for school leaders. Principals understand that at the end of the day, they need to figure out how to help teachers improve their instructional practice; however, the sheer number of demands on their time have made the job untenable for many leaders. This leadership challenge led the Center for Educational Leadership (CEL, 2012) to develop the 4 Dimensions of Instructional Leadership framework. Based on research and what we have learned from our work in the field, the framework is not the sum total of everything a principal must do to be successful, but it is a description of the most salient practices of instructional leadership linked to the improvement of teaching and learning.

The 4D framework (Table 2.1) identifies high-impact practices that are organized within 4 dimensions and 10 subdimensions. (A detailed examination of the framework is presented in Figure 2.1 at the end of this chapter and is also available online at https://www.K-12leadership.org/4d.) In what follows, we take the reader into the 4D, zooming into the case of Mountain View Middle School to illuminate the high-impact instructional leadership practices identified in the 4D.

### Vision, Mission, and Learning-focused Culture

This dimension is foundational to effective instructional leadership and is organized in two subdimensions: *vision and mission* and *learning-focused culture*. Instructional leaders consider how they might accomplish the following:

- Engage staff, students, and the school community in developing a vision and mission that provide a clear direction for academic success for every student.
- Align stakeholders' decisions and actions to the vision and mission of the school and demonstrate a growth mindset.

**Table 2.1**
**The 4D framework**

| DIMENSION | SUBDIMENSION |
| --- | --- |
| Vision, mission, and learning-focused culture | • Vision and mission<br>• Learning-focused culture |
| Allocation of resources | • Marshaling resources<br>• Deploying resources |
| Management of people and processes | • Talent management<br>• Professional growth<br>• Structures of support |
| Improvement of instructional practice | • Shared vision of effective instruction<br>• Observation and analysis<br>• Support for teacher growth |

- Establish measurable goals aligned to the vision and mission of academic success for every student.
- Engage with stakeholders to foster culturally responsive learning that ensures individual students' learning needs are met.
- Create and maintain a results-focused learning environment based on clearly established data-driven goals that underscore high expectations for every student and every adult.

Instructional leaders ask themselves these questions:

- What does the school's environment and day-to-day interactions among students, staff, and families say about what is valued in the school community?
- How do we communicate and drive the school's instructional agenda?
- How is the learning environment organized to respond to diversity, for example, race, class, language, disability, and the varying learning needs of students?
- How do we use evidence of student success to continuously drive improved achievement?

- How do we develop and encourage leadership within others to support and drive the vision, mission, and culture of learning throughout the school?

- How do we use data to instill urgency around student learning and the role of a learning-focused culture in improving student achievement?

**Laying the Foundation**  Similar to all such frameworks, the 4D's statements and descriptors depict an ideal state, a North Star to help guide instructional leadership decisions. As an experienced leader, Rachel understands that she has to take a longer, iterative view of vision, mission, and culture building, tending to "first things first." That first step is engaging the school community in developing a vision and mission that provides a clear direction for academic success for every student. This step is extra important given that Mountain View Middle School houses a district-wide program for gifted and talented students along with the neighborhood students who come from several feeder elementary schools. Rachel is committed to creating a school culture in which teachers constantly collaborate to solve problems of student learning for *all* students, not one in which only the gifted students are expected to excel.

With the support of the district (discussed in greater detail in Chapter 7), Rachel had a full planning year prior to the opening of the school. She used this time well to jump-start the creation of a school-wide vision and mission. Rachel started with the community early on—as soon as the boundaries were set—working with the elementary feeder schools. She met with families from each of the feeder school communities and asked them these questions:

- What do you want to see in your child's education?

- What's the best part of the schools that your children attend now or have attended?

- What are the lessons that we can learn as we open our school?

From these initial meetings, Rachel created a parent advisory board with representatives from each of the feeder elementary schools.

About the same time, in January of the year leading up to the fall opening of Mountain View Middle School, Rachel was able to hire a core team of teachers to help with the planning process. It was a small group of six—five teachers and a guidance counselor. Rachel noted, "They did their homework on me. I did my homework on them, so we were able to start to develop a mission and vision for the school in which instructional practice and embedded professional development were key elements before we even started." While Rachel engaged this core team in shared vision and mission building, she also brought her vision to the table, which included her deeply held values and non-negotiables. For example, Rachel had a strong vision of what professional development would look like based on her prior success creating a culture of public practice in which professional learning was authentically embedded into the daily work of teachers. She understood that student learning needs would be met only when teachers continually and collectively work to deepen their own expertise and improve practice. This way of working became a staple part of the Mountain View Middle School culture, which you will see in subsequent chapters.

**Building on Common Ground**  With the foundational work underway to establish a vision and mission that provided a clear direction for academic success, Rachel worked over the next three years to forge and codify a learning-focused culture. Reflecting on year one, when she needed to focus on the technical aspects of opening a school, she said, "There's a ton of that technical stuff that just had to be taken care of, and that first year I constantly talked about Maslow's hierarchy of needs, such as we need to be safe. Such as you all need to know that when you call the office someone's going to be sitting at that desk." But at the same time, she also pressed on three learning-focused questions:

- What do we expect to see in the classrooms?
- How do we get some consistency throughout the school?
- What specific goals do we want in place, and how will we go about measuring our improvement?

The very essence of *culture* means that it had to embody the entire school—students, teachers, and staff members. As such, from the outset, Rachel has worked with her core team of teachers to become "instructional council leaders," so they can collectively engage with the entire staff in the codification of the vision and mission, including the establishment of learning-focused norms and ensuring that those norms were well socialized throughout the school. Members of the instructional council did not have prior experience as department chairs or prior leadership roles, but Rachel wanted to rely on their shared leadership and supported and coached the teacher leaders as they worked and learned with their colleagues.

Rachel and her instructional council members have worked to define and codify the instructional vision and create the learning-focused culture through multiple strategies, including modeling. They seize every opportunity with staff members as a venue to model best instructional practice, to pose authentic questions the school has surfaced, and to bring forward particular students—their strengths and needs—as a focal point for inquiring into practice. Rachel understands that everything is connected to everything else, so whether dealing with a technical issue such as the establishment of safety drills or discussing instructional strategies, each time the staff members are together is a time to model and reinforce the vision, mission, and learning-focused culture. The learning-focused culture at Mountain View Middle School has evolved and deepened during Rachel's leadership tenure. By the end of year three the entire staff is engaged in looking at multiyear data to determine the instructional focus for the following year, and, increasingly, Rachel and her assistant principals are having conversations with teachers with disaggregated data in hand.

Establishing a vision, mission, and learning-focused culture is not a one-time event. It is a perpetual way of working, paying constant attention to student learning and how the adults in the school collectively strive to get better on behalf of the students in their charge. Staff turnover, changes in the student population, and the development of increasing levels of expertise all can influence the culture in ways that prompt a constant reexamination. Rachel constantly sets expectations, reinforces new learning, models her own learning, and focuses on the norms of practice that would continue to bring the school ever closer to their vision.

## Allocation of Resources

This dimension is organized into two subdimensions: *marshaling resources* and *deploying resources*. Under *marshaling resources* instructional leaders consider how they might do the following:

- Use data of student learning and teacher practice, aligned with the school's vision and mission, to determine needs.
- Identify and leverage the resources of time, money, technology, space, materials, expertise, and partnerships innovatively and equitably for maximum benefit to all students.
- Creatively and proactively access additional resources that support strategic priorities.

Under *deploying resources* instructional leaders consider how they might do the following:

- Articulate clear decision-making processes and procedures for instructional programming and the equitable allocation of resources.
- Plan for and align resources to support the implementation of instructional initiatives.

- Use a continuous cycle of analysis with leadership teams to examine, assess, and refine the effectiveness of programs and equitable use of resources.

Instructional leaders ask themselves these questions:

- How is the equitable distribution of resources (e.g., time, money, technology, space, materials, and expertise) related to improved teaching and learning in this school? What evidence do you have?
- How do school leaders use instructional coaches, mentors, and other teacher leaders to help improve instructional practice?
- How do school leaders address gaps in resources?
- How do school leaders make decisions about staff allocation and interventions to ensure that the varying needs of students are met? Who participates in decision-making?
- How do school leaders use staff time and collaborative structures to drive the instructional program?
- How does the school schedule support the needs of all students?
- What evidence exists that the school leaders prioritize time for the improvement of teaching practice and student learning?
- How does the leadership team monitor and adjust implementation plans?

**Marshaling Resources** In the planning and opening of Mountain View Middle School, Rachel was able to marshal a variety of resources to support the school's instructional vision. During the planning year, prior to the opening of the school, Rachel worked hard to organize and empower her prospective school community of parents and other stakeholders to guide and support her efforts. She mobilized a cadre of parents and community members with varying areas of expertise to volunteer at the school. Volunteers provide a wide range of supports including administrative, tutoring, and technology. Rachel reached out to the local university to recruit faculty members with expertise and research interests that might help with specific instructional improvement efforts.

Rachel worked with the district to ensure that ample funding was allocated for planning purposes, which included the early hiring of her instructional council members. There were several different sources of district funding, and not only was Rachel vigilant in ensuring that Mountain View Middle School received an equitable amount of funding but also she worked hard to establish maximum discretion in the deployment of those funds. Even within traditional federal and state categorical funding, Rachel was savvy enough to understand that there is often more flexibility in the use of those funds than the district categorical administrator would offer. Rachel was not afraid to ask tough questions and push on the system in assertive but positive ways to meet the instructional improvement needs of her school.

**Deploying Resources**   Principals receive budgets, generally on a formula basis, allocated from the district. And as we have seen, entrepreneurial principals marshal other kinds of resources as well (i.e., time, money, technology, space, materials, and expertise). Ideally, principals use data to make equitable decisions regarding the allocation of these resources in a way that is aligned with their overall vision, mission, and improvement goals. This was certainly the case at Mountain View Middle School.

One of the early resource deployment decisions Rachel made with her teachers was for a schoolwide advisory program. This was especially important given that the school housed neighborhood students and the district-wide gifted and talented program. Rachel knows the importance of creating one, diverse school as opposed to two separate entities. She understands that it is crucial for students to have opportunities to know each other's stories and strengths. Rachel recalls having to work strategically with staff members, community, and families to build support for initiatives such as an integrated advisory program, while also working to understand what the different stakeholders want for their students.

Although Rachel has a variety of district discretionary budget allocations to support her instructional improvement work, her district labor contract stipulates that the school budget has to pass by two-thirds of a staff vote. This requires Rachel to continually refer to the school vision and mission for the principles that ground the school's collective budget decisions. In general, over four years, Rachel and her staff members have had discretion over the deployment of approximately $300,000. The teachers referred to this as their "equity dollars," because (1) those dollars have been generated on a weighted student staffing formula so that students who qualify for free and reduced lunch generate even more dollars and (2) because they have done so much early work in establishing an equity-driven school vision and mission.

With equity as the foundational cornerstone, ample student performance data in hand, and well-defined problems of teaching practice identified through teachers' professional learning communities (PLCs) and learning walks, Rachel has no problem meeting the two-thirds voting threshold to make the following deployment decisions:

- Lower the size of math classes.
- Create positions for two veteran teachers to have a coaching period a day in math (and one in literacy).
- Deploy mentor teachers by reducing some teachers' schedules by one or two periods a day.
- Contract for outside professional development support from the local university to support math professional development.
- Support teacher release time to participate in learning cycles.

## Management of People and Processes

The dimension of *management of people and processes* is organized into three subdimensions: *talent management, professional growth,* and *structures of support.* Under *talent management* instructional leaders consider how they might do the following:

- Use data to establish priorities for recruiting, selecting, inducting, supporting, and developing staff.
- Engage in ongoing succession planning.

Under *professional growth* instructional leaders consider how they might do the following:

- Create and maintain supportive working environments with time and space for collaboration.
- Identify and provide multiple types of professional development based on identified needs.

Under *structures of support* instructional leaders consider how they might do the following:

- Employ critical processes such as planning, implementing, advocating, supporting, communicating, and monitoring of all leadership responsibilities, including curriculum, instruction, assessment, and school improvement planning.
- Use data to assess and monitor system performance on a regular basis to ensure viable support for staff and students.

Instructional leaders ask themselves these questions:

- What evidence exists that the school leadership implements strategic efforts to recruit, hire, retain, induct, support, develop, and evaluate staff?
- How do school leaders use the evaluation process to make personnel decisions?
- What data and processes does the school leadership use in planning for instructional and school improvement?
- What evidence is there of a comprehensive assessment system?
- What evidence exists of staff access to professional growth opportunities?
- How is the leader using performance management systems for staff growth?
- How do leaders establish structures to support critical processes such as curriculum development, comprehensive assessment, school improvement, and performance management?

**Talent Management**   One of the most important roles principals play is to ensure they have the right people in their schools to carry out the jobs that need to be done. Instructional leaders have to be very strategic in their recruitment and hiring. They have to be very strategic in onboarding newcomers and developing staff members. And they have to be mindful of retirements and other unavoidable attrition so that they can plan well for succession.

Rachel understands that the ongoing development of a learning-focused culture begins with the hiring process. Hiring staff members with personal beliefs and values aligned to the school vision is an important start. A critical first step for the principal to know when hiring teachers is knowing their teaching strengths and weaknesses. Rachel has designed an interview process that requires candidates to teach a lesson. The interview team (consisting of teachers and other staff members) use their teacher evaluation rubric as a way of assessing the candidate's knowledge, skills, and expertise. Over time not only does the interview team become more sophisticated in how they might score their potential future colleagues but also the interview process provides a valuable opportunity to reflect on their own individual teaching practice. Rachel also understands the importance of developing future leaders, perhaps providing a succession path for assistant principal positions. Teachers have opportunities to develop their leadership expertise through a number of school structures that included PLCs, the instructional council, the advisory design committee, and a parent-community advocacy design group. Teachers can also become mentors and instructional coaches for their teaching colleagues. Over time, the math teacher leaders, for example, have taken increasing responsibility for planning and leading professional learning with their consultant, Andrea.

Rachel also works closely with her assistant principals to develop and hone their instructional leadership skills. Each week they spend time together in classrooms calibrating their observations and then discussing potential next steps for how they can support a given teacher. They engage in common book reads and develop and share individual learning plans. Rachel understands her role as principal is to build the capacity of her assistant principals so that they can one day become a school principal.

**Professional Growth**   We have already discussed Rachel's strong vision for authentic, embedded professional learning as a way of working at Mountain View Middle School. The next chapters are designed to illustrate how that vision plays out in specific ways. We show that the principal's job is to create a supportive working environment with time and space for collaboration. We have seen that collaboration is a hallmark of Mountain View Middle School. For Rachel, the idea of collaboration isn't a "must" because of some language in the teachers' contract. Collaboration is actually a deeply held value with the understanding that the best way to unlock human potential is by creating opportunities for staff member synergy. Rachel understands that practice does not improve in isolation.

**Structures of Support**   Principals have to manage all kinds of processes. Think about all of the school improvement initiatives that exist and the role of instructional leaders to make sense of all those initiatives. How do leaders make certain that staff members understand how the initiatives at the district level and the initiatives in the school are integrated, how they are aligned, and how they are all going to contribute to the overall mission and vision of the school? This does not happen by accident, and it is why the designers of the 4D framework took a broader view of instructional leadership. The ability (including expertise, time, and space) to be in classrooms with teachers does not happen by accident or in isolation. There are critical systems management functions that must be attended to so that there is alignment of and coherence across the school.

Rachel has thoughtfully designed various structures and processes to develop a shared vision, mission, and learning-focused culture. She has allocated resources in service of establishing and growing this culture, and she has managed people and processes in alignment with growing this culture.

## Improvement of Instructional Practice

This dimension is organized into three subdimensions: *shared vision of effective instruction, observation and analysis,* and *support for teacher growth.*

**Shared Vision of Effective Instruction**   In *shared vision of effective instruction* instructional leaders consider how they might do the following:

- Use an instructional framework to establish a common language and shared vision of effective instruction.
- Ensure that content standards drive instruction.

**Observation and Analysis**   In *observation and analysis* instructional leaders consider how they might do the following:

- Use an instructional framework to observe and analyze teaching practice.
- Use instructional practice data to engage staff in the assessment and improvement of teacher and leader practice.
- Use classroom observation data to determine next steps for instructional leadership practice.

**Support for Teacher Growth**   In *support for teacher growth* instructional leaders consider how they might do the following:

- Support teacher growth using ongoing feedback, professional development, coaching, and professional learning communities.
- Use evidence of student learning to plan and implement individual and whole-staff professional development.

Instructional leaders ask themselves these questions:

- How do we use observational data and student learning products to identify trends in teacher practice and student performance to determine problems of learning?
- How can we use an instructional framework to observe, analyze, and give feedback to the whole staff and individual teachers about instructional practice?
- How do we use instructional practice and student learning data to identify, plan, implement, and assess all types of professional development?

- How do we use an inquiry- and strengths-based stance to give feedback to teachers about instructional practice?

- How do we use cycles of inquiry to identify professional development needs and grow teaching practice?

The vision statements and guiding questions in this dimension are always on Rachel's mind as she engages the staff members in the early vision and mission work. Rachel understands the symbiotic relationship among the dimensions of *vision, mission, learning-focused culture,* and the *improvement of instructional practice* of the 4D framework. She can't engage in the deep improvement work found in the *improvement of instructional practice* dimension without establishing a strong vision, mission, and learning-focused culture. At the same time, Rachel's vision of instructional improvement, particularly how to support teacher learning, is a strong guidepost from the beginning so that the early vision and mission worked can be grounded to a vision of high-quality teaching and learning.

In the next few chapters, we illuminate the dimension of the *improvement of instructional practice* through our case study. We invite readers to consider the guiding questions for this dimension as the chapters explicate the processes and tools Rachel and the teachers engage with at Mountain View Middle School. As you read the case study, note Rachel's skill for observing and analyzing teaching and learning and how she organizes useful learning opportunities and feedback for the math department. Indeed, although all four dimensions of the 4D are equally critical, the dimension of the *improvement of instructional practice* requires the deepest development of a leader's instructional expertise. In this case, you will note that the nature of Rachel's engagement with the math department and leadership team enables her to continually develop her own instructional expertise.

## DISCUSSION QUESTIONS

1. What are the instructional leadership practices your district prioritizes?

2. Understanding that the development of a deep learning-focused culture is an iterative process that is cultivated over time, how do you figure out what to do first, second, and third and with what urgency?

3. How might you think more broadly and creatively about the resources necessary for school improvement?

## REFERENCES

Jerald, C. D. (2012). *Leading for effective teaching: How school systems can support principal success.* Seattle, WA: Bill & Melinda Gates Foundation.

Supovitz, J. A., & May, H. (2011). The scope of principal efforts to improve instruction. Educational Administration Quarterly, 47(2), 332–352.

University of Washington Center for Educational Leadership (CEL). (2012). *4 dimensions of instructional leadership.* Seattle, WA: Author.

---

### Figure 2.1
### 4 dimensions of instructional leadership™: Instructional leadership framework 2.0

Among school-related factors, school leadership is second only to teaching in its potential influence on student learning. Instructional leadership is a critical component of school leadership. The work of instructional leaders is to ensure that every day, in every classroom, every student has a powerful learning experience. Doing so requires that instructional leaders *lead for the improvement of instruction and the improvement of student learning*. This framework is not the sum total of the work of instructional leaders. Rather, it is a description of the most salient aspects of instructional leadership. Five core beliefs undergird the concepts of this framework and therefore drive our school leadership work here at the Center for Educational Leadership.

**Instructional leadership:**

1. Is learning-focused, strengths-based and measured by improvement in instructional practice and in the quality of student learning.

2. Must reside with a team of instructional leaders of which the principal serves as the "leader of leaders."

3. Requires a culture of public practice and reflective practice.

4. Must address the cultural, linguistic, socioeconomic and learning diversity of the school community.

5. Is grounded in the relentless pursuit of equity and the use of data as levers to eliminate the achievement gap.

---

**Figure 2.1**
*(continued)*

| 4D™ | SUBDIMENSION | THE VISION | GUIDING QUESTIONS |
|---|---|---|---|
| Vision, Misson and Learning-focused Culture | Vision and Mission | • Engage staff, students and the school community in developing a vision and mission that provide a clear direction for academic success for every student.<br><br>• Align stakeholders' decisions and actions to the vision and mission of the school and demonstrate a growth mindset. | • What do the school's environment and day-to-day interactions among students, staff and families say about what is valued in the school community?<br><br>• How do school leaders communicate and drive the school's instructional goals?<br><br>• How do school leaders organize the learning environment to respond to diversity (e.g., race, class, language and disability) and the varying learning needs of students? |
| | Learning-focused Culture | • Establish measurable goals aligned to the vision and mission of academic success for every student.<br><br>• Engage with stakeholders to foster culturally responsive learning that ensures individual students' learning needs are met.<br><br>• Create and maintain a results-focused learning environment based on clearly established data-driven goals that underscore high expectations for every student and every adult. | • How do school leaders and the school community use evidence of student success to continuously drive improved achievement?<br><br>• How do school leaders develop and encourage leadership within others to support and drive the vision, mission and culture of learning throughout the school?<br><br>• How do school leaders use data to instill urgency around student learning and the role of a learning-focused culture in improving student achievement? |

*(continued)*

**Figure 2.1**
*(continued)*

| 4D™ | SUBDIMENSION | THE VISION | GUIDING QUESTIONS |
|---|---|---|---|
| Improve-ment of Instructional Practice | Shared Vision of Effective Instruction | • Use an instructional framework to establish a common language and shared vision of effective instruction.<br>• Ensure that content standards drive instruction. | • How do school leaders use observational data and student learning products to identify trends in teacher practice and student performance to determine problems of learning?<br>• How do school leaders use an instructional framework to observe, analyze and give feedback to the whole staff and individual teachers about instructional practice?<br>• How do school leaders use instructional practice and student learning data to identify, plan, implement and assess all types of professional development?<br>• How do leaders and teachers use an inquiry- and strengths-based stance to give feedback to teachers and leaders around instructional practice?<br>• How do school leaders and teachers use cycles of inquiry to identify professional development needs and grow teaching practice? |
| | Observation and Analysis | • Use an instructional framework to observe and analyze teaching practice.<br>• Use instructional practice data to engage staff in the assessment and improvement of teacher and leader practice.<br>• Use classroom observation data to determine next steps for instructional leadership practice. | |
| | Support for Teacher Growth | • Support teacher growth using ongoing feedback, professional development, coaching and professional learning communities.<br>• Use evidence of student learning to plan and implement individual and whole-staff professional development. | |

| 4D™ | SUBDIMENSION | THE VISION | GUIDING QUESTIONS |
|---|---|---|---|
| Allocation of Resources | Marshaling Resources | • Use data of student learning and teacher practice, aligned with the school's vision and mission, to determine needs.<br><br>• Identify and leverage the resources of time, money, technology, space, materials, expertise and partnerships innovatively and equitably for maximum benefit to all students.<br><br>• Creatively and proactively access additional resources that support strategic priorities. | • How is the equitable distribution of resources (e.g. time, money, technology, space, materials and expertise) related to improved teaching and learning in this school? What evidence do you have?<br><br>• How do school leaders use instructional coaches, mentors and other teacher leaders to help improve instructional practice?<br><br>• How do school leaders address gaps in resources? |
| | Deploying Resources | • Articulate clear decision-making processes and procedures for instructional programming and the equitable allocation of resources.<br><br>• Plan for and align resources to support the implementation of instructional initiatives.<br><br>• Use a continuous cycle of analysis with leadership teams to examine, assess and refine the effectiveness of programs and equitable use of resources. | • How do school leaders make decisions about staff allocation and interventions to ensure that the varying needs of students are met? Who participates in the decision making?<br><br>• How do school leaders use staff time and collaborative structures to drive the instructional program?<br><br>• How does the school schedule support the needs of all students?<br><br>• What evidence exists that the school leader prioritizes time for the improvement of teaching practice and student learning?<br><br>• How does the leadership team monitor and adjust implementation plans? |

(continued)

**Figure 2.1**
*(continued)*

| 4D™ | SUBDIMENSION | THE VISION | GUIDING QUESTIONS |
|---|---|---|---|
| Management of Systems and Processes | Talent Management | • Use data to establish priorities for recruiting, selecting, inducting, supporting, evaluating and developing staff.<br>• Engage in ongoing succession planning. | • What evidence exists that the school leadership implements strategic efforts to recruit, hire, retain, induct, support, develop and evaluate staff?<br>• How do school leaders use the evaluation process to make personnel decisions? |
| | Professional Growth | • Create and maintain supportive working environments with time and space for collaboration.<br>• Identify and provide multiple types of professional development based on identified needs. | • What data and processes does the school leadership use in planning for instructional and school improvement?<br>• What evidence is there of a comprehensive assessment system?<br>• What evidence exists of the staff's access to professional growth opportunities? |
| | Structures of Support | • Employ critical processes such as planning, implementing, advocating, supporting, communicating and monitoring of all leadership responsibilities including curriculum, instruction, assessment and school improvement planning.<br>• Use data to assess and monitor system performance on a regular basis to ensure viable support for staff and students. | • How is the leader using performance management systems for staff growth?<br>• How do leaders establish structures to support critical processes such as curriculum development, comprehensive assessment, school improvement and performance management? |

# The Role of Observation in Supporting Teachers' Learning

Let's return to Rachel, the middle school principal, and her mathematics leadership team. Rachel gathers her team in her office: Nadia, the assistant principal who supervises mathematics, and Sadie and Diane, the two veteran math teachers who are also released one period a day to provide coaching to their colleagues. It is September of the fourth year of Mountain View Middle School's existence. The math department has added two new teachers, and there are five returning staff members just launching their school year with a diverse group of young adolescents and preadolescents. Of the five returning staff members, three are in their first three years of teaching. The school has grown in size and the classrooms have become increasingly dynamic and complex. As they convene, Rachel reminds the group that student academic discourse in classrooms is a school-wide focus: in addition to their department professional learning work last year, this fall there had been some school-wide professional development already designed to help teachers increase the amount of student talk across the content areas. The team gathers around two large pieces of chart paper and starts reviewing the school's professional learning goals from last year.

Recall that the math professional development had focused on discourse in math classrooms and helping teachers to analyze what students say to formatively assess what they understand. This work has helped the teachers see that, with support, more students could discuss what they are learning and trying to figure out, and that they could gain valuable insight into their students' thinking by listening in to their discussion—rather than waiting for a final assessment. Across the year, the team has learned about the complexity of what it takes to create classrooms where students can use and own mathematical academic language to describe their thinking and reasoning. In order to help the teachers get a picture of what discourse in math can look like, and in order to give them the opportunity to inquire together as they tried out new practices, the math consultant, Andrea, has used a professional development structure known as *studio*. This structure involves Andrea guiding the teachers and leaders through a collaborative planning process resulting in a lesson, supporting the team in teaching the lesson in a classroom together while participants observe and collect data, and then conducting a discussion of what students have learned and the associated teaching practices. The studio classroom is akin to an artist's studio, where teachers can try on new ideas, apply new practices with support, and try out new ways to interact together as professionals. (For a more elaborated explanation of the studio, please see our first book, *Leading for Instructional Improvement* [Fink & Markholt, 2011], or Gallucci, Van Lare, Yoon, and Boatright [2010]). The teachers reported that the professional learning has been relevant and helpful. However, although Rachel sees some change in her two most-experienced teachers' rooms, Rachel is not convinced that the majority of the classrooms are changing. On multiple occasions, she has observed her lead teachers facilitating whole-class discussions of complex problems and inviting students to share their thinking with partners or in small groups. She has also seen them creating charts while having discussions in order to capture students' thinking and language (Figure 3.1). In other classrooms, Rachel has noted that teachers posted more charts with phrases to guide student talk (Figure 3.2).

However, she was still seeing teachers doing most of the talking and then having students work independently. Similar to us, Rachel believes that for professional learning to be considered effective, there has to be observable change in practice over time resulting in observable improvements for student learning.

Entering the fourth school year, Rachel has two big questions:

- To what extent and how are the different math teachers implementing the professional learning goals for student talk and formative assessment of student talk?

- What does the level of implementation suggest about next steps for the department's learning?

## Figure 3.1    Teacher-created charts to prompt discussion

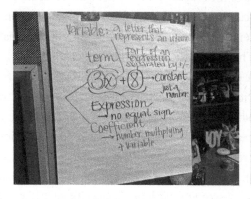

## Figure 3.2    Strong mathematicians ask probing questions

**Strong Mathematicians Ask Probing Questions**

- What steps did you do?
- Can you sketch an example?
- Why did you choose _____?
- I agreed with _____ because _____.
- How did you know what to do?
- Where did the _____ come from?
- Is your answer reasonable?

These questions ground the leadership team's classroom visits today. Rachel knows the group needs to collectively examine what is happening in mathematics instruction and to start to develop a plan for the department's learning for the year. This work sits inside the *improvement of instructional practice* dimension of the 4D framework, specifically the *observation and analysis* subdimension. Rachel knows that engaging the whole team, including teachers, in this process will ultimately lead to a more informed decision about the direction, and she models a process of co-inquiry in the leading of instruction.

After all, the teachers know the students best. Rachel comments to the team, "We have a sense that the brand-new teachers, and some of the second-year teachers, are struggling to implement what they are learning in the recent math professional development sessions. They have too many classroom management struggles." Nadia, the assistant principal, nods, and adds, "They are trying, though. That's what we want to check out today. We all want to see what they have been trying in the past few weeks and ask ourselves what next?" Of course, the purpose of this walk is not to judge the teachers. The purpose is to see what teachers are already doing and to look for what they might be close to trying next—all in service of helping teachers get better at increasing students' engagement in mathematics. You may want to read more about the different purposes of classroom learning walks in our previous book (Fink & Markholt, 2011). Rachel and her team are about to engage in what we refer to as an *implementation and goal-setting walkthrough*. (See Table 3.1, at the end of this chapter, for descriptions of the various types of walkthroughs.)

The group starts by reviewing the professional learning goals from last year and what they might expect to see based on those goals:

- All math teachers will implement structures and processes to develop and support mathematical discourse, to create anchor charts, and to create public records of student thinking.

- Math teachers will develop collaborative norms and processes for examining and interpreting formative student learning data (including charts, records of student discourse, and student journals) in order to plan for instruction.

The team has found that reviewing goals and discussing specific look-fors help them to calibrate a vision for student talk in mathematics. The conversation enables them to synthesize and review their own learning about math instruction. Without this step, the leadership team members may have different ideas about what they are looking for—different definitions and expectations of math discourse and formative assessment. Over time, the team members have found their ideas have been challenged and have grown. They have developed more-sophisticated mental representations for what math discourse sounds like and what formative assessment looks like and are able to be more specific now than they were a year ago. Today, Rachel makes notes on the large chart paper to create a record of the group's thinking. This time, they agree they will be looking for teachers engaging in the following activities:

- Teachers creating situations in which students are required to talk about math. Teachers will provide students tasks that require collaboration to complete them, for instance, providing just one slip of paper or providing different group members different pieces of information or different tools or manipulatives.

- Teachers providing sentence stems or anchor charts to support student academic vocabulary development and students using them to talk to each other. Students will independently (or in small groups) reference these charts and stems for support when they are reaching for a word or idea.

- Students pressing each other for clarification and justification, asking each other, "How do you know that works?" "Does that work every time?"

- Teachers listening to partners talking about math and taking notes on what students are saying and adjusting as the lesson proceeds. Teachers may say, "I am noticing some of you are trying . . . so now I will . . ."

Yet, as they make their way toward the first classroom, Rachel reminds her team that "we may see that, we may not. Right now, we are just going to observe." This reminder helps the group discern between talking through their vision to calibrate and the development of their ability to just *see*—to develop the discipline to see strengths, potential, and what the individual teachers are approximating. Rachel's team has worked hard to stay committed to observing through this lens of what teachers *are* doing and not their deficits. In the early days of their work as a team, Nadia and the teacher leaders would observe classrooms and feel constantly disappointed, describing their frustration that teachers were not doing *more* to implement their learning. In turn, their disappointment got in the leaders' way as they tried to provide effective feedback that could help teachers improve. Furthermore, the teacher leaders needed practice and support in how to observe in their colleagues' classrooms. Unlike formal leaders such as principals, teacher leaders may have had limited exposure to the skills of taking descriptive, low-inference data when observing. Rachel has helped her team maintain a strengths-based stance, prompting them to start by naming what is in place and look for the next entry point just beyond where teachers are right now.

## WHY OBSERVATION OF TEACHING AND LEARNING MATTERS

As leaders, it is our role to recognize the complexity of what happens in classrooms, and it is our responsibility to support teachers as they take risks and implement what they are learning. In order to know what is happening and what is possible, we must observe classrooms as often as we can. You will find that throughout this book, we start with the foundational work of observing instruction. Just as teachers use formative assessment to guide their teaching, formative observation plays a role for leaders in all stages of professional development, informing our ability to plan and adjust along the way. As previously mentioned, the 4 Dimensions of Instructional Leadership describes this work inside the *improvement of instructional practice* dimension. Leaders use collaborative observation and analysis of instruction as a way to gather and then analyze data that will inform collective decision-making about next steps for leadership. Furthermore, this observation process allows Rachel and her team to plan for *support for teacher growth,* including using evidence of student learning to plan and implement individual and whole-staff professional development. You will also notice the use of an instructional framework to ground these conversations. The conversations that follow in this chapter help illuminate what leaders might do to create a shared vision of effective instruction as they build a common language through calibration and observation.

However, we also know from experience that observing teaching and learning is a complex process. Many of us remember being observed by principals as teachers and recall receiving feedback that felt judgmental—in positive or negative ways—and often without specific evidence. In the era of teacher evaluation reform, principals have been learning to collect unbiased evidence of classroom practice, and yet we have a long way to go. Many teachers and leaders still mentally link all observation with evaluation and judgment rather than with evidence collected in service of growing teacher and student learning. Rachel, Nadia, Sadie, and Diane have been actively working on observing classrooms in service of seeing what is happening—a habit and discipline that we find leads to more trust and collective investment in the complex work of developing teaching practice in service of students. Indeed, research suggests that frequent observation leads to less apprehension for observation (Marzano, Frontier, and Livingston, 2011).

The Mountain View team is about to engage in a highly complex process—observing teaching and learning through the lens of their professional development goals, keeping a stance that embraces what is possible and what is already happening, and applying their growing content expertise to their observation and analysis. We have already mentioned that over the year of professional learning, the team's expertise has grown, enabling them to be more specific about what to look for. They know more about what student-to-student talk in math looks and sounds like. This growing expertise helps them observe with more nuance and sophistication as their mental representations expand. We find that as teachers and leaders develop increasing expertise in a content area, including how students come to learn it and how teachers learn more sophisticated ways to teach it, then the more expansive our observation and analysis will be. As we gain more expertise, we bring more nuance to bear on the complicated work of supporting teacher learning. For instance, when we observe a classroom where a teacher previously has not had students talk about their thinking but is now starting to provide sentence stems to support student talk (e.g., "I noticed . . . so what do you think about my idea?") and assigning partners for quick conversations, our expertise helps us recognize this practice as an early step in a teacher's journey to increasingly sophisticated practices in supporting student talk. We will then be able to consider what this teacher's next step toward supporting longer, more elaborated discussions might be. Expertise to observe and analyze teaching and learning is truly a discipline and stance as well as a skill.

## USING THE 5 DIMENSIONS OF TEACHING AND LEARNING (5D) TO ANALYZE TEACHING AND LEARNING

Many districts across the country have adopted instructional frameworks as a way to build a common language and vision for high-quality teaching and learning. An instructional framework can be a tool that can help anchor observations and discussions of classrooms. The 5 Dimensions of Teaching and Learning (5D) is one such framework. In our first book, *Leading for Instructional Improvement,* we elaborate more on the history of the framework and how systems are using it to support calibration and analysis of teaching and learning. Since the writing of our first book, our framework and accompanying performance assessment has undergone a four-year validation study by researchers at the University of Washington and Vanderbilt University. The first phase of this federally funded study reaffirmed that these five dimensions indeed capture a broad and important range of instruction for leaders to notice in classrooms. (To read more about this study and the Measures of Instructional Leadership Expertise (MILE) assessment, please see http://info.K-12leadership.org/mile-assessment.)

## HOW THE 5 DIMENSIONS OF TEACHING AND LEARNING INSTRUCTIONAL FRAMEWORK IS ORGANIZED

The 5D is organized into five dimensions, each with a set of subdimensions. The framework summarizes the aspects of instruction that expert observers attend to: *purpose, student engagement, curriculum and pedagogy, assessment for student learning,* and *classroom environment and culture.* The framework also includes vision statements that describe what that dimension looks and sounds like in an ideal state and a set of guiding questions that can prompt leaders to attend to what they may otherwise miss or to deepen their ability to reflect and see.

The 5D framework helps leaders build expertise, develop their ability to see patterns, and supports their skills in posing questions before drawing conclusions. The framework directs leaders' attention to important aspects of instruction, supporting their ability to stay descriptive and specific in the observation and analysis process. Let's join Rachel, Nadia, Sadie, and Diane as they enter Samantha's seventh-grade classroom and then step out with them as they process what they saw.

## Samantha's Seventh-Grade Classroom

When the group enters the room, they see students talking at their tables with partners. They are all seated in groups of two or three with tables facing the front of the long and wide room. Samantha, a second-year teacher, is circulating around the room. The team moves closer to student pairs to hear what students are talking about and what they are doing. As they look closely at the students' desks, they see that they have one number line per pair on their desks with positive and negative integers up to 10 in each direction. The question on the board is as follows:

1) What do we remember about adding negative and positive numbers? What do we remember about multiplying and dividing negative numbers? Solve: $-5 + 5 =$ *and* $-5 \times 5$.

The group notes that the students are talking, to varying degrees, about the question that is on the board.

On the walls, there are charts with definitions and examples of terms such as *negative integer, positive integer, opposites, real numbers.* Another chart states, "Ask your partner to justify by saying, 'Why do you think that? Does that always work?'" On the white board, the teacher has indicated today's learning goal is "Students will discuss and apply their understanding of positive and negative integers and how to combine them."

One girl tells her partner, "negative numbers plus positive numbers . . . it is like subtracting." The partner looks away and then replies, "Can you show me? I think it has something to do with hops on the number line, remember?" The first student says, "I don't remember."

At another table, we notice a pair of boys who are English language learners. They have, in addition to the number line, some manipulatives in two different colors that sit in three piles in front of them. The boys are stacking the manipulatives and looking up at the charts on the wall with the language support. One boy says to his partner, "How do we know that this is right? These blue ones are supposed to be positive and the red ones are supposed to be negative, right?"

Another pair of boys is discussing how to use the number line to show adding 5 to −5. They seem to agree on how to represent the solution as 10 and after a few moments they start talking about lunch.

We notice Samantha stops to listen in on this second pair's conversation. She says, "How do you know that you have solved this problem correctly? What did you try?" They look at her blankly. She pauses. "You know on Facebook when you post something and someone posts a sad face? That's like a negative. Other people may post smiling faces or thumbs up. That's like a positive. What if five people said they didn't like something you posted and then five more said they did?" The boys look at each other and then one says, "It's like 0! The likes and dislikes cancel each other."

## Analyzing Their Data: Noticing, Wondering, Using the 5D

After visiting several classrooms, Rachel and her team return to her office. They start by reviewing the goals and the look-fors. They note that the goals for the math department spread across all five interrelated dimensions of the 5D. For instance, students need to know the purpose of their discourse, and the prompts for discourse need to be tied to grade-level standards and tasks. In order to have discussion, students need to have supports for their participation and meaning-making in the classroom, which are forms of student engagement. This discourse requires a particular classroom environment and culture with norms that allow students to test out ideas and take risks. Likely, some students will need scaffolds and disciplinary-appropriate supports to engage in discussion. These pedagogical strategies are captured in the curriculum and pedagogy dimension of the 5D. The extent to which teachers listen and respond to the discourse is reflected in *assessment for student learning*. While the leaders focus their debrief on the professional development goals in a holistic way, we separate their discussion into five broad areas aligned with the 5D—*purpose, student engagement, curriculum and pedagogy, assessment for student learning,* and *classroom environment and culture.*

What follows is a description of how the team analyzed what they noticed and wondered with respect to the department goals—through the lens of the 5 Dimensions of Teaching and Learning. The process of *noticing* is really the act of describing in neutral terms the current state of instruction with respect to the goals. We include a column below that reflects the team's questions, or *wonderings,* as well. These are questions that may arise inside the observer's mind as a result of that observer's expertise and genuine curiosity about the decisions a teacher is making. For instance, asking "Have you ever considered posting the learning target with a graphic to support the students?" is an example of making a suggestion cloaked as a wondering. However, asking "How do you make decisions about when and how to share the learning goal with students?" is an example of a question that would elicit potentially helpful information about teacher knowledge and thinking. The team may or may not ask these questions of the teachers to gather more data. These questions in and of themselves are not feedback; they are a way of observing and processing while assuming positive intent on the part of the teacher. We know from the research that expertise affects not only what we notice but also the questions we pose, the analysis we engage in, and the theories and hypothesis we develop about what we notice. We conclude with their thoughts about the strengths and possible next steps (*verges*) in this classroom. This is the same process the group repeats for each classroom they visit as they analyze their formative data.

**Purpose**   In order to consider what students are asked to talk about and how they are asked to talk about it (*the task*), Rachel and her team think about what they see in terms of lesson purpose. They consider the extent to which the lesson is tied to grade-level standards or some larger purpose beyond the day's lesson. Although it has not been the deliberate focus of their professional learning, the team has come to realize that some of the teachers are teaching below expectations in grade-level standards. Given the range of learners in their classrooms, the team now understands that part of the reason for this discrepancy is that teachers are not sure *how* to engage the range of students in the rigorous content, including connecting it to their background knowledge and experiences. In the case of mathematics, the leaders are particularly concerned with the rigor of the tasks students are asked to discuss, specifically the extent to which these tasks include opportunities to develop mathematical reasoning (thought processes used by mathematicians such as representing quantities using symbols and manipulating the symbols), conceptual understanding (comprehension of mathematical concepts, operations, and relations), as well as procedural fluency over time. The team acknowledges that in the past, as is the case in much of the country, their instruction—and any student discussion—has focused on procedures alone (the algorithms students can use to solve problems quickly and efficiently but often without understanding) (see the Common Core Standards of Mathematical Practice and the National Research Council's report *Adding It Up* [Kilpatrick, Swafford, & Findell, 2001]). They recognize that a single lesson may be focused on a procedure (and, indeed, the standards expect students to learn certain procedures) but that over time students experience performance tasks that also prompt them to discuss their developing concepts, their approaches to complex problems, and their mathematical reasoning. So, with these ideas in mind, consider what the team notices and wonders.

| THE TEAM NOTICES . . . | THE TEAM WONDERS . . . |
| --- | --- |
| • The lesson's learning target—Students will discuss and apply their understanding of positive and negative integers and how to combine them—is related to a seventh-grade standard regarding rational numbers. It is also procedural. | • What the teacher understands about what it means to apply understanding of positive and negative integers and how to combine them and what about that skill is the goal for today. What will students do next? |
| • The mathematical learning target is posted on the board. | • Over time, to what extent are the tasks for discussion *procedural* in nature? |
| • The students have a verbal and written task that asks them to describe what they know in general about combining and multiplying positive and negative numbers and are given an example of each. | • What would it look like for the students to be successful in this lesson with this task? |
| • Samantha stops and talks to a partnership about their answers and when they cannot justify their thinking, she provides them with an example that seems to connect with something students already know (Facebook). | • How does the teacher make decisions about helping students know what success looks like? |
| | • How does the teacher make decisions about how and when to have students talk about their learning as part of the task of the lesson? |

**Student Engagement**   As they continue to analyze what they see, the team pauses to consider the level and quality of student engagement in the classrooms. They consider what they have been learning about discourse in math classrooms, including the kinds of talk and meaning-making that are valued in the discipline. For instance, mathematicians talk about alternate strategies for solving problems and how the mathematics underlying these strategies connects. Some of their professional learning focuses on the idea that through structured discussion opportunities, teachers can create opportunities for students to press each other's explanations, probing for alternate strategies, explanations, and mathematical arguments (Kazemi & Stipek, 2001) rather than accepting one response and strategy or accepting one "right" answer and dismissing "wrong" ones. This type of press represents the authentic, intellectual work of the discipline of mathematics and ultimately becomes internalized by students in their individual work. As students are supported to talk *more* and in mathematical ways, they learn to think more like mathematicians, practicing engaging in the Standards for Mathematical Practice, such as Constructing Viable Arguments and Critiquing the Reasoning of Others (CCSS.Math.Practice.MP3 at www.corestandards.org/Math/Practice/#CCSS.Math.Practice.MP3). Furthermore, reflecting on the struggles that some students face when learning mathematics through traditional means, the teachers also try different engagement strategies to scaffold students' ability to take part in discussions. The result of these efforts, the teachers come to understand, would be the creation of more-equitable classrooms where all children can develop more positive, empowered identities as students who can *learn* math (Boaler, 2013; Cobb, Gresalfi, & Hodge, 2009). The following table summarizes the team's related observations and questions.

| THE TEAM NOTICES . . . | THE TEAM WONDERS . . . |
| --- | --- |
| • The students have been asked to think about and discuss what they already know about combining positive and negative integers and they have a sample problem to discuss. This task requires students to consider what they know and apply it—in some way—to some integers. In the time provided, some students use academic language to discuss what they know, and one student asks another student to explain, showing some basic ownership of the learning and thinking. Other students finish the discussion without pressing each other before time is up.<br><br>• The turn-and-talk strategy enables students to discuss the questions with one another. The teacher refers to Facebook as a strategy to help one partnership connect their thinking to an experience they already have had.<br><br>• The posted chart has academic language for the unit and prompts such as, Ask your partner to justify by saying, "Why do you think that? Does that always work?" *could* support students to discuss their thinking with each other. I notice one student ask a partner, "Can you show me?" but the student's partner is not yet able to carry on the conversation from there. | • How does the teacher select tasks for discussion? To what extent does she consider the amount of meaning-making required?<br><br>• What does Samantha notice about the students' ability to carry on a conversation about mathematics at this point? What does she notice about their level of justification and ability to press? |

**Curriculum and Pedagogy**   Rachel and her team also think about the curriculum and pedagogy associated with the lesson in order to understand the discussion and assessment opportunities. When examining the instructional approaches, they consider the extent to which the teachers demonstrate mathematical content knowledge and knowledge of how students come to learn math. They consider the extent to which a teacher uses instructional materials and tasks that are relevant, rigorous, and aligned to the learning goals as well as to the broader unit or concept under study. They reflect on the three-part lesson structure they have learned as part of their professional development: launch, explore, summarize (Van de Walle, Karp, & Bay-Williams, 2013). In this approach, the teacher first presents a problem but does not show students how to solve it (*launch*). Then, during the *explore* phase, the students are expected to generate ideas, create and test conjectures, and create mathematical arguments and counterarguments rather than having the teacher demonstrate a process and expect them to repeat it. Teachers can formatively assess the students during the explore phase by listening to their conversation and watching them work. They also understand that during the *summarize* phase, students potentially might be asked to summarize their ideas and build on each other's thinking, or the teacher might strategically sequence the order of student responses to show the development of an idea or strategy. Furthermore, they consider the specific supports or scaffolds the teachers uses to build student understanding and thinking. The following table summarizes the team's collective observations and wonderings.

| THE TEAM NOTICES . . . | THE TEAM WONDERS . . . |
|---|---|
| • The prompt for student discussion observed is related to the content area standards.<br><br>• The vocabulary chart in the room suggests that the students are in the midst of a unit (vocabulary is relevant to the topic: *integer, positive, negative*). The learning target states, "Students will discuss and apply their understanding of positive and negative integers and how to combine them," making the team wonder where this lesson fits in the sequence—it seems to be a review.<br><br>• In terms of materials, the students have number lines that are also relevant to the content as a whole and the specific concept under study.<br><br>• There is a chart on the wall with two sentence prompts students can use to ask each other to justify their thinking. The concept of justification is important in mathematics and has been a focus of the professional development.<br><br>• The teacher did ask one group some questions ("How did you know that you solved this problem correctly? What did you try?") about their thinking rather than correcting their misunderstanding right away. | • How does the teacher want the students to discuss and apply the concept of positive and negative integers to ideas they already have?<br><br>• If this was the explore phase, what did the teacher notice and then decide to highlight in the summarize phase?<br><br>• What is the teacher's vision for students using these charts and scaffolds in discussion? How does she make decisions about what to represent publicly on charts?<br><br>• How does the teacher typically structure lessons and how does this snippet fit?<br><br>• How does the teacher decide when to prompt and when to correct? What does she believe about incorrect answers? |

| THE TEAM NOTICES . . . | THE TEAM WONDERS . . . |
|---|---|
| • The charts and the number line are scaffolds to help students build the concept of positive and negative integers and how to combine them. The ELL students we observe appear to have been looking to the charts, but it is unclear how they are using them and how they are using the additional manipulatives they have. | • How does Samantha choose which tools to provide which students? What does she notice about the ELL students' use of their tools and what does she want for them? What is she trying out with them? |

**Assessment for Student Learning** Rachel and her team also consider the opportunities for teacher and student assessment and then teacher adjustments of instruction based on what they see in student learning. As a math department, the teachers are learning how to assess the students while they discuss and grapple with problem-solving during turn-and-talk partner discussions or small- and large-group discussions. At first the teachers are tempted to correct students' thinking as it emerges during opportunities for discussion or charting. Andrea shows the teachers research that argues instead that in order to build student independence they instead focus on listening carefully, constantly assessing, offering suggestions only as needed (Van de Walle, Karp, & Bay-Williams, 2013). The group analyzes the classroom data considering the opportunities for teacher assessment (not evaluation!), adjustments to instruction that appeared to occur as a result, and any chances for students to assess their own learning. The following table summarizes their thinking.

| THE TEAM NOTICES . . . | THE TEAM WONDERS . . . |
|---|---|
| • Samantha circulates the room while students are talking, which *might* indicate she views student talk as a source of information about them. The topic of the turn-and-talk conversation matches her goal for the lesson, so this might indicate she has created this moment to assess their understanding of the learning goal.<br>• Samantha listens to one partnership who has reached an incorrect conclusion about −5 + 5. She asks them two questions about their process that they could not answer, and then she provides them with an example that appears to help them clarify. This could be an adjustment. | • What did Samantha notice as she circulated?<br>• How does she choose and design questions for discussion that she intends to use for assessment?<br>• How (if at all) does she collect information about her students' thinking?<br>• What did Samantha notice about this partnership? How does she decide when to probe, when to provide other ways of thinking, and when to correct? |

**Classroom Environment and Culture**    As they talk, Rachel and the math team think a great deal about the classroom environments and cultures in the classrooms they observe. They know that if *all* students are to be able to talk about and take ownership of their mathematical thinking, classrooms would have to be physically arranged to support their ability to see and hear each other. Furthermore, the *classroom environment and culture* dimension of the 5D prompts them to think about their learning about the routines in the classroom. For instance, knowing that many students do not see themselves as capable of mathematical reasoning, they consider the extent to which the classroom routines help students to own their own ideas as opposed to deferring to the teacher or one or two students (Boaler, 2013; Dunleavy, 2015). They wonder what the classroom routines (such as asking for help, collaborating on an assignment, verifying answers) communicate about who has the knowledge in the classroom. They also consider the norms in the classroom about discussion, norms that Yackel and Cobb (1996) argue are particular to math (socio-mathematical norms), such as the notion of using errors to reexamine a problem and propose alternatives and working individually and collaboratively in a group—and reaching consensus through mathematical argument. Finally, knowing the importance of the teacher's role in orchestrating classrooms that support this level of student ownership and independence, they analyze the responses teachers offer students, how they set up the discussions, and how they set up the tasks. The following table summarizes their thinking.

| THE TEAM NOTICES . . . | THE TEAM WONDERS . . . |
|---|---|
| • Students are seated in pairs—an arrangement that is appropriate for this partner discussion. All students can see the prompt and the charts and have the number lines on their desks, which enables them to complete the task today.<br><br>• All students are talking with their partners when prompted, which is evidence that students likely have routines for talking in pairs. Some pairs are less successful in sustaining conversation than others.<br><br>• Samantha approaches two students who have reached an incorrect answer—and she discusses their answer with them neutrally, first offering them the chance to explain their thinking before jumping in with an example. This move positions the students as thinkers and collaborators rather than as passive listeners. | • How are students typically seated? To what extent does the teacher make decisions about how students are seated based on the learning goals?<br><br>• How does Samantha make decisions about partner talk supports? What is her vision for how students participate in these pairs?<br><br>• What is her vision for student-to-student discussion of responses when there is no agreement on an answer or process? |

Rachel and her team repeat this process to debrief each of the five classrooms they visit. They aim to develop clarity on what the teachers are learning—how they are interpreting and processing the professional learning in the mathematics classrooms—and use the 5D to support their analysis. Their goal is not to say that it is or is not happening but to discuss *how* teachers are implementing or approximating implementation of new learning. Collecting and sharing low-inference data (*noticing*) is the foundation of this work because it provides a source of information about what is happening now with regard to the focus. When leaders can maintain an inquiry stance toward what they see (*wondering*), they are also in a better position to understand teacher thinking and intention than they would be if they jumped to solutions and conclusions prematurely. Leaders ultimately internalize this process, but the discussion and charting that Rachel's team use also reflect a habit of leadership that allows for group problem-solving and a degree of calibration. The 5 Dimensions of Teaching and Learning framework guide their analysis, serving as a conceptual map to expand the breadth and depth of their collective noticings and wonderings.

## Examining the Trends: Strengths and What Are We on the "Verge Of"?

After Rachel's team complete this discussion of each of the classrooms visited, they pause and step back to discuss what they have been noticing across the classrooms. Now Rachel asks the team, "What are we already doing well? What are the *strengths* in the math department right now considering our goals? And, what are we on the *verge of*?" This process enables the leaders to describe the current state first— rather than starting with a corrective stance and a discussion of deficits. Rachel and her team then share these trends in strengths with the department. By focusing on what the department is on the verge of—what they are approximating and what they are ready to do next with support—the group begins to think about next steps within reach. These observations may ground the professional development goals for the year. The team also discusses these ideas with Andrea, the consultant working with them. The department chairs (Sadie and Diane) ask the teachers for input. The following list summarizes the strengths and verges the group discusses and charts.

| STRENGTHS ACROSS CLASSROOMS | VERGES ACROSS CLASSROOMS |
|---|---|
| • There are charts in classrooms with academic language specific to the unit of study.<br>• Students are being asked to talk to their partners to explain their thinking, often using language such as "help me see your thinking . . ." or "how did you decide to use that strategy?" or "does that always work?"<br>• Students are talking to partners when prompted.<br>• Students are working in groups or pairs to solve problems of varying degrees of complexity—some tasks have only one clear way to solve them.<br>• Teachers are providing manipulatives to students to aid in understanding.<br>• Teachers are asking students to justify (explain why).<br>• Students are trying out the language of justification. | • Some teachers provide some tasks that allow for discussion—teachers are on the verge of offering more complex tasks but may not be sure how to do so.<br>• Students are starting to try out the language of justification—they could be supported to use this language and do this thinking more regularly. Students are ready to have a more active role in thinking about and responding to each other's thinking with scaffolding. |

## LOOKING AHEAD

Much of the rest of this book is focused on three main roles for principals in the leadership of professional learning—determining specific outcomes, sponsoring, and following up. All three roles depend on regular, thorough, and formative observation and analysis of classroom practice. As we describe in this chapter, in order to observe classrooms well, we know that leaders need to practice taking a nonjudgmental, descriptive stance—one that searches for what is happening rather than what is not happening. We also know that through repeated observation, use of an instructional framework, and participation in professional development for teachers, principals develop increasing levels of expertise that enable them to see *more* in classrooms, ask better questions, and analyze more thoroughly. We have also learned that the more expertise we have, the better we are at asking questions about what we see, noticing trends across classrooms, and organizing support for teacher learning.

## DISCUSSION QUESTIONS

1. How often do you visit classrooms with your leadership team? What is your purpose for these observations?

2. To what extent do you and your leadership team use your instructional framework as a tool to observe and analyze classrooms together? What other tools do you use?

3. What is next for you in terms of your observation and analysis process?

## REFERENCES

Boaler, J. (2013). Ability and mathematics: The mindset revolution that is reshaping education. *FORUM, 55*, 143–152.

Cobb, P., Gresalfi, M., & Hodge, L. (2009). An interpretive scheme for analyzing the identities that students develop in mathematics classrooms. *Journal for Research in Mathematics Education, 40*(1), 40–68.

Dunleavy, T. K. (2015). Delegating mathematical authority as a means to strive toward equity. *Journal of Urban Mathematics Education, 8*(1).

Fink, S., & Markholt, A. (2011). *Leading for instructional improvement: How successful leaders develop teaching and learning expertise.* San Francisco, CA: Jossey-Bass.

Gallucci, C., Van Lare, M., Yoon, I., & Boatright, B. (2010). Instructional coaching: Building theory about the role and organizational support for professional learning. *American Educational Research Journal, 47*(4), 919–963.

Kazemi, E., & Stipek, D. (2001). Promoting conceptual thinking in four upper elementary mathematics classrooms. *Elementary School Journal, 102*, 59–80.

Kilpatrick, J., Swafford, J., & Findell, B. (Eds.). (2001). *Adding it up: Helping students learn mathematics.* Mathematics Learning Committee, National Resource Council. Washington, DC: National Academy Press.

Marzano, R. J., Frontier, T., & Livingston, D. (2011). *Effective supervision: Supporting the art and science of teaching.* Alexandria, VA: Association for Supervision and Curriculum Development.

Van de Walle, J. A., Karp, K. S., & Bay-Williams, J. M. (2013). *Elementary and middle school mathematics, teaching developmentally, the professional development edition for mathematics coaches and other teacher leaders.* New York, NY: Pearson.

Yackel, E., & Cobb, P. (1996). Sociomathematical norms, argumentation, and autonomy in mathematics. *Journal for Research in Mathematics Education, 27*(4), 458–477.

## Table 3.1
## Types of classroom observations

| TYPES OF OBSERVATIONS | PURPOSE(S) | SUPPORTING THEORY | LOGISTICAL CONSIDERATIONS | POSSIBLE LEADERSHIP ACTIONS FOR CONSIDERATION |
|---|---|---|---|---|
| **Learning Walkthrough**<br><br>District administrators, principals, and teacher leaders focusing on one or more dimensions of instruction (e.g., student engagement, curriculum and pedagogy, and the like), connected to an identified problem of leadership practice | • To develop a shared vision for high-quality teaching and student learning based on an instructional framework (e.g., 5D)<br><br>• To calibrate and deepen understanding of the dimensions of an instructional framework (e.g., student engagement and classroom environment and culture)<br><br>• To calibrate understanding of "best practices" in a particular content area<br><br>• To provide principals and teacher leaders a tool to assess their own classrooms against an emerging vision of instruction<br><br>• To begin to use the language of an instructional framework to communicate learning to staff members<br><br>• To develop a school and district culture of "public practice"<br><br>• To gather data necessary to identify relevant problems of practice<br><br>• To observe and analyze the impact of teacher practice on student learning | • If we (as school and district leaders) spend regular and focused time in classrooms observing and describing teaching practice with the support of an instructional framework, then we will develop a common vision and shared understanding of high-quality instruction and how it affects student learning.<br><br>• If we develop a common vision and shared understanding of high-quality instruction, then we will be able to identify and lead with greater clarity the improvement of teaching practice.<br><br>• If we are open and transparent about our own learning, then we will be able to model the kind of reflective learning culture necessary to support improved practice for all. | • Who will participate?<br>• Which classrooms will we visit?<br>• How much time will we spend in classrooms?<br>• What protocols, tools, or processes will we use in classrooms?<br>• What data will we collect?<br>• What protocols, tools, or processes will we use after the walkthroughs to gather feedback and to inform next steps?<br>• What and how will we communicate to staff members? | How will you do the following?<br><br>• Communicate with staff members about the walkthrough.<br>• Model what it means to be a learner.<br>• Highlight and celebrate what you want to reinforce.<br>• Use teacher expertise to build collective learning.<br>• Use your deepened understanding of quality instruction to inform critical problems of leadership practice.<br>• Strategically plant seeds for future dialogue and reflection.<br>• Articulate your vision for teaching and learning.<br>• Consider revisions to professional development plans for individuals and groups.<br>• Provide an avenue for feedback and conversation on the process and subsequent learning. |

*(continued)*

**Table 3.1**

*(continued)*

| TYPES OF OBSERVATIONS | PURPOSE(S) | SUPPORTING THEORY | LOGISTICAL CONSIDERATIONS | POSSIBLE LEADERSHIP ACTIONS FOR CONSIDERATION |
|---|---|---|---|---|
| **Goal Setting and Implementation Walkthrough**<br><br>District level: central office leaders, principals, teacher leaders<br><br>School level: principal, instructional coaches, teachers | • To determine the level of implementation of curriculum materials and guidelines along with further support and professional development needed to implement the curriculum with fidelity<br><br>• To determine the extent to which new learning(s) resulting from specific professional development offerings are being applied in actual practice<br><br>• To determine additional supports and/or professional development needed to implement learning(s)<br><br>• To establish the school instructional improvement goals<br><br>• To determine schoolwide patterns across grade levels and subject areas to inform professional development<br><br>• To determine individual goals and supports for teachers<br><br>• To monitor student progress<br><br>• To help identify a problem of leadership practice | • If we carefully monitor the expected level of implementation of new curriculum and/or professional development learning(s), then we will be able to measure the level of implementation across the district and/or school.<br><br>• If we are able to identify the level of implementation of new curriculum and/or professional development learning(s), then we will be in a position to bring focused and differentiated support where necessary to improve the implementation and/or application of new practices.<br><br>• If we examine our teaching practices in light of our deepened understanding of powerful instruction, then we will be able to establish specific improvement goals (district, school, or individual) along with the professional development necessary to improve practice. | • Who will participate?<br>• Which classrooms will we visit?<br>• How much time will we spend in classrooms?<br>• What data will we collect?<br>• What and how will we communicate to staff members?<br>• What protocols, tools, or processes will we use in classrooms?<br>• What protocols, tools, or processes will we use after the walkthroughs to gather feedback and to inform next steps? | How will you do the following?<br><br>• Communicate with staff members about the walkthrough.<br>• Highlight and celebrate what you want to reinforce.<br>• Create and communicate new expectations if necessary.<br>• Use teacher and principal expertise to build collective learning.<br>• Modify professional development as needed.<br>• Strategically consider providing new and/or additional supports, for example, professional development, coaching, study groups, readings, and so on, if necessary.<br>• Articulate your vision for teaching and learning.<br>• Provide an avenue for feedback and conversation on the process and subsequent learning. |

| TYPES OF OBSERVATIONS | PURPOSE(S) | SUPPORTING THEORY | LOGISTICAL CONSIDERATIONS | POSSIBLE LEADERSHIP ACTIONS FOR CONSIDERATION |
|---|---|---|---|---|
| **Supervisory Walkthrough**<br><br>Supervisors and principals | • To examine the teaching and learning process as it relates to the school's and district's instructional goals<br>• To examine relevant student performance data and monitor student progress<br>• To focus on progress made since the last walkthrough visit and the best type(s) of professional development to meet teachers' needs<br>• To identify specific leadership actions necessary to support the improvement of teaching practice<br>• To assess leader's understanding of new learning<br>• To hold leaders accountable for agreed-on leadership actions | • If we carefully examine and monitor student performance data and the quality of teaching and learning in light of our deepened understanding of powerful instruction, then we will be able to identify specific leadership actions necessary to improve practice.<br>• If we carefully examine and monitor the extent to which agreed-on leadership actions are enacted, then we can hold leaders accountable for the improvement of teaching and learning. | • What student performance data will we examine?<br>• Which classrooms will we visit?<br>• How much time will we spend in classrooms?<br>• How often should we visit specific classrooms?<br>• What other school structures will we observe, for example, department meetings, PLC meetings, and so on?<br>• What will we communicate to staff members?<br>• What protocols, tools, or processes will we use in classrooms? | How will you do the following?<br>• Communicate with staff members about the walkthrough.<br>• Highlight and celebrate what you want to reinforce.<br>• Create and communicate new expectations if necessary.<br>• Provide new and/or additional supports, for example, professional development, coaching, and so on, if necessary.<br>• Articulate your vision for teaching and learning.<br>• Hold leader(s) accountable for agreed-on actions.<br>• Assess the implementation of agreed-on actions using student learning as a measure. |

# Planning for Focused Professional Learning

As Rachel, the principal, and her team complete their analysis of their math department observations, they start to reflect on the next question, "Now what? And why?" In other words, the discussion turns to the professional learning goals, purpose of those goals, and the support plan for the current school year. This chapter illustrates what principals might do, in collaboration with their leadership teams, to plan for professional development for the school. In the 4 Dimensions of Instructional Leadership, this work sits inside the *improvement of instructional practice* dimension, including the *observation and analysis* and the *support for teacher growth* subdimensions. Notice how the leadership team as a whole uses student learning data, instructional practice data, and observation data to begin to plan for goals for individual and whole-group professional learning. Also note reference to multiple types of professional learning, including formal professional development, coaching, feedback, and PLCs.

Sadie and Diane, the department cochairs, start discussing how they are happy to see that teachers are trying more student engagement strategies than they had expected, despite what they have been hearing about classroom management struggles. They acknowledge that there is a range of what teachers have been implementing, but that as a whole, the trends they identify apply across the group. They also remind each other that this year they have more time in their schedules (a full period a day each) to coach teachers—and this means more support, so possibly they can expect more progress. After listening to the team for a few minutes, Rachel suggests that the group step back a bit and decide what they want to discuss with the department and with their math consultant, Andrea. She asks the team to consider what kind of input they need now to make a good decision about their focus this year. Also, what do they want to see in student learning as a result of this learning? Rachel says, "One thing I have learned this year is that we have to be very clear about where we are going as a department—and also why."

As previously mentioned, the Mirage report (The New Teacher Project, 2015) identifies several reasons that professional development typically has a relatively low impact on teaching practice. One important reason is a lack of clarity about what successful practice looks like. We find that leaders might not necessarily have the expertise to know what kinds of changes in instruction are needed and what kinds of changes in student learning are appropriate and reasonable to look for after professional development has occurred. It is typical for leaders to express goals that are too vague or too ambitious. We might want "all third graders reading at grade level" after a year's professional learning about close reading. We might want "increased equity" in classrooms, or in Rachel's case, increased access to grade-level mathematics. These are indeed important and compelling goals, but they may not be helpful in guiding the day-to-day problem-solving, planning of professional development, planning for follow-up, or the analysis of success. If we are to expect teachers to learn and make change in their practices, we as leaders need to know what those changes will look like and how *we* will support their growth in that direction. Planning effective professional development requires many skills by instructional leaders. Leaders have to consider the context, identify the need, and structure the professional development so that the learning is clear and implemented effectively. To support this analysis, we provide a tool we call *planning for focused professional learning* (see Table 4.1 at the end of this chapter). We designed and refined this tool through our work with principals, coaches, and district leaders as we worked together to create purposeful professional development.

What follows in this chapter is an elaboration of the thinking and analysis that the Mountain View Middle School math leadership team (including lead teachers, assistant principal, and principal) conducts with input from the rest of the math department and the math consultant, Andrea. We begin with a narrative description of the team's thinking as they move through the tool. We have learned that over time, outcomes and plans become increasingly refined. To illustrate this point, we include completed *planning for focused professional learning* templates from a third year of math work at Mountain View and also the parallel literacy work the school began in its second year of professional development. These examples can be found in Table 4.2 and Table 4.3 at the end of this chapter.

## CONSIDER THE CONTEXT

At their next leadership meeting, the Mountain View math leadership team takes Rachel's suggestion into thorough consideration. They gather in the conference room with all their learning walk data, some recent student math assessment data, and their planning for focused professional learning tool. To begin, they ask themselves, What are we really grappling with as a department? What is the problem we are trying to solve? The team wants their colleagues to understand that the professional learning would again be a year-long opportunity to grapple with and improve in the complex and sophisticated work of teaching the students in their classrooms to think and talk like mathematicians. They know that, fundamentally, there remain persistent gaps in performance and that ELLs in general are not passing the state math assessments. But this divide in test scores in and of itself does not alone constitute enough impetus for collective problem-solving in their grade-level meetings or eagerness for external input in the math department. They recall how at the start of the previous year the teachers had been a bit suspicious of the arrival of a consultant in their August math department convening. At that time, the teachers were new to thinking of themselves as learners on a trajectory of practice. The leaders acknowledge that the department has shifted this year but that framing the year's work with specific rationale would continue to be important.

Sadie comments that she realizes now that her previous experience teaching in a high-performing middle school has not prepared her to teach math at Mountain View Middle School. "Here, you have to know how to reach students with very diverse math backgrounds." She comments that this school year, with the decision to place all students in integrated seventh-grade math classes ("de-tracking" them), students who had been sorted into classes by perceived ability now share the same classroom. She comments that her colleagues, whose backgrounds are similar to hers, have received fairly traditional preparation as math teachers and that many of them have chosen middle school math teaching as a profession because they themselves love the content of secondary math—and had been successful math students themselves. "Last year," Sadie continues, "was the first time I really stopped and listened to how my English language learners talked about their reasoning—and it was eye-opening to see what they could do if I gave them that extra space to talk. At the same time, I had students such as Olivia in my class, who spent half the summer at robotics camp and would check out if it seemed we were going too slow. That's hard! Unless you teach all eighth-grade honors classes, no one has classes of just *Olivias* this year. And, I don't want that type of class!"

Rachel nods and says, "Yes, I am hearing one huge piece of the context here is that we know we have a gap in student performance in our school, especially with our ELL students, and that we are learning how to create opportunities for them all to perform day-to-day in the classroom. This will be a problem of practice for *all teachers* because everyone will have at least one class that is de-tracked. How does that fit with where we are with academic talk and formative assessment in math?" The team returns to the trends they collected in their visits to classrooms during their previous meeting.

Diane comments, "Well, we are seeing that, based on what we learned last year in our professional development, we are getting more students talking in class. That gives us the chance to hear what they are all thinking and adjust our teaching. And we are creating more charts with student language and support for students to talk. So, there is evidence we are trying on what we learned in one year."

"I don't want to lose ground. I can see teachers might lose some of these habits—we are still fragile in some ways as a department. We can't go in a totally new direction already . . . *and* we have new textbooks this year," Sadie adds. "None of us knows how to figure out how to use them. What will that do for discussion in our classrooms? I can see us going back to just having students fill in worksheets!"

Rachel nods, taking notes, and summarizes, "So, we have a start on getting more students to talk more in class, and we are even posting student thinking on charts now in our rooms as a support for them. And, we have the added layer of a new textbook—which could be very helpful for us—we just don't know yet." Finally she asks, "Why is any of this context important?"

The team pauses again and starts talking about who the teachers in the department are. They acknowledge that again they are going to be grappling with how to support some first- and second-year teachers with running their classrooms successfully as well as developing some teachers who are entering their third year and are deciding whether or not to stay in teaching at all. Diane and Sadie look at each other and Nadia says, "the students can't wait for us to get a stable teaching staff together. We have to teach these students *now*. This year feels like it could be a turning point if we can create a department in which the teachers truly collaborate and work together to support all our kids—and a department where we look to Andrea to help us build our vision and support us when we are stuck and are not sure what to do next."

Rachel nods. "Yes. I can't wait for us to figure out together how to raise expectations and access for students to develop as mathematical thinkers in all of our classes and to support each other along the way."

## IDENTIFY THE NEED

Having clarified the context of the professional learning, the team turns its attention to what the specific teacher practice needs are. Rachel comments that she has identified several needs and asks the team to think about the highest priorities. She also notes that this is where they might need input from the department as well as from Andrea.

Diane comments, "I think we still don't know how to plan for student discussion opportunities that are meaningful. I can get my students to talk but it sometimes falls flat, and I don't know how to set them up to talk about their thinking—not just their procedures." The group agrees with Diane and the group starts discussing *what* students are discussing in classes. They acknowledge that sometimes students are just being asked to report out their answers rather than talk to develop thinking—and sometimes it seems that the tasks set up for discussion do not actually prompt very much thinking.

Nadia agrees and adds, "I also see that sometimes when teachers ask their students to talk about a problem, the teacher just stands there at the front of the room. Don't they want to know what the students are saying? That makes me wonder if they know *why* they are asking students to talk and how they can improve the students' discussion. And then there's the new curriculum. I keep coming back to that, too."

The group summarizes these needs for planning toward student talk and what to do during student talk and the potential impact of trying to figure out the new curricular resources. Then, they look at one another. Rachel asks, "What would the other math teachers say are their needs?" The group remembers that they had engaged in a self-assessment as a department at the beginning and end of the previous school year using the same questions. They recall that at the start of the year they had all said they routinely create classroom tasks and discussions that involve active meaning-making and support meaningful learning rather than getting the right answer, but at the end of the year, they all rated themselves as only sometimes doing that (Figure 4.1). It seems that as the department has learned more throughout the year, they have a better sense of their own needs. Rachel suggests that now that the new year is just getting going, they conduct the self-assessment again and see what teachers say. "We could add some questions, such as 'What makes it challenging to create these tasks?'"

The group agrees that this is a good next step. They also decide that they need support from Andrea to determine, specifically, what aspect of the need would be the highest leverage focus.

**Figure 4.1**
**The department's self-assessment**

Do we record students thinking so that we can develop metacognitive awareness and monitor learning & performance?

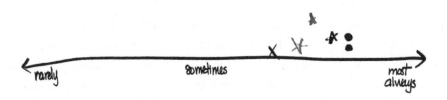

rarely        sometimes                    most
                                           always

- Co-created anchor charts ✓✓✓✓
- student-led discussions around student mistakes & strategies. ✓✓
- focus on error analysis → "what does this tell me about myself as a mathematician?"
- Exit ticket analysis ✓
- write down student responses during student discussions whether its correct or incorrect
- photos of board, copy student work to analyse

**Figure 4.1**

*(continued)*

Do we provide opportunities for students to explore complex tasks that may include multiple approaches or answers that are not immediately apparent so that students can meaningfully organize their knowledge and apply to new situations?

rarely                              sometimes                    almost
                                                                always

• On some content better than others. Sometimes it's great, sometimes not. Need to get more consistent.

- when presenting new content, provide a task that students can draw previous knowledge ✓

• I want to do this more, it happens in some units but not consistently. ✓

• Several very successful times this year, will build on for next.

- Number talks
- Choosing their favorite strategy
- Students share multiple ways of how they solved a problem

*(continued)*

**Figure 4.1**
*(continued)*

Do our classroom tasks and discussions focus on student's thinking that involve active meaning making and supports meaningful learning rather than just on getting the right answer?

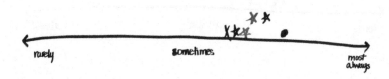

rarely                    sometimes                              most
                                                                 always

- analyzing common mistakes (ex. exit tickets) ✓
- Give the answer, ask for the Question
- Student co-created anchor charts emphasize Strategies
- Questions phrased "how?✓ why?... when?..."
- "Other answers/solutions?"
- "How would someone have gotten ___?" What mistake are they making? How can we explain what they are doing?"
- Provide time for multiple solutions to be shared, as mistakes come up in class have students contribute to what the error was + how we can learn from it.

**Figure 4.1**
*(continued)*

Do we routinely ask students to talk and question each other as they solve problems? Do we construct knowledge socially through meaningful discourse?

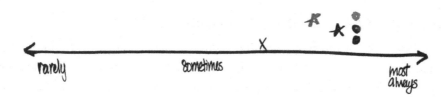

rarely · · · · · sometimes · · · · · most always

- Students are given time to respond to each other: ask questions, build on thinking agree (support w/evidence or restate) or disagree (support w/evidence). ✓✓
  - small group modality
  - fish bowl
  - *sentence starters
  - Pair shares
  - asking for point + care of other
- students routinely volunteer to answer questions posed to teacher → and they critique each others reasoning with an eye on the math ✓
  - others respond or question ✓✓

"Very good at student presentations for small parts of lesson... can it be more consistent?
- Number talks

A week later, armed with results of the teachers' own self-assessments and notes from a conference call with Andrea, the team has a clearer sense of what, specifically, the need is for the year. The teachers are asking for help with using the curriculum materials—especially what to prioritize in them. They also need help knowing what to do when students get stuck but the curriculum tells them it is time to move on. The leadership team starts to understand that the quality of student talk will not improve in the classrooms until the teachers have a better understanding of how to prioritize specific math goals based on their standards and their students' needs, how to use the curriculum materials as a base for choosing or adapting complex tasks that require students to struggle and justify their thinking, and how to actively listen to how students talk and make meaning of math during these tasks.

## ARTICULATE CLEAR TEACHER AND STUDENT OUTCOMES

Now that they have a better handle on the need, the math leadership team knows it is time to clarify the specific goals for the department's learning. They plan to get input from the staff members on these goals, but they also know that the rest of the teachers will not necessarily have the expertise to draft them on their own. Rachel comments that they have already learned so much about the importance of specific goals for professional learning. She recalls that at the start of last year, before arriving at their outcomes, they started with something too big and broad to visualize, measure, and support.

The group practices drafting language to describe what the teachers will be learning *and* how that learning will reach the students in the classroom. They agree that this step of their process forces them to slow down and be specific about the end game. As Sadie notes, "We do this as teachers all the time. We have to know where we are trying to go with our students if we are going to plan a daily lesson."

After a few revisions, the group arrives at these three outcomes. Notice that the first outcome is similar to the first outcome from the previous year. The group also decides that although they want to see results in *all* students' performance, their data suggests the ELLs in the de-tracked seventh-grade math classes require particular attention:

- All math teachers will continue to learn structures and processes to develop and support mathematical discourse, to create anchor charts, and to create public records of student thinking, *which will result in* all students participating in written and verbal discussions that require them to argue mathematically and justify their thinking, particularly seventh-grade ELLs.

- All math teachers will learn to prioritize math goals and design correlating mathematical tasks that have multiple ways to solve them, *which will result in* all students (focus on seventh-grade students and ELLs) participating in discussions that require them to argue mathematically and justify their thinking. A measurable number of students will transfer these skills into their independent problem-solving.

- All math teachers will learn how to analyze student talk during these tasks, *which will result in* students understanding that they talk about math in order to explore, generalize, and develop justifications—not to just be "right."

## ARTICULATE EXPECTATIONS FOR IMPLEMENTATION

Using the *planning for a focused professional learning tool* as the guide, Rachel and her team know that in order for the professional learning of the year to be successful, Rachel will have to be clear with herself, her team, and the math department in general about what the teachers are expected to implement. Without this clarity, teachers might experience their time with Andrea as a series of isolated events. Rachel asks, "Our goals are ambitious, and I know we can do it. But, what will this reasonably look like this year? What will be *better* by the end of the year in teachers' planning and in their instruction? How will we know they are better at doing it?"

Sadie, Diane, and Nadia agree that this step is a bit challenging because they have not yet experienced the professional development. We find that as leaders develop their expertise through content area professional development, they may refine their expectations. In other words, they are asking themselves to articulate goals without a clear vision for what will be possible. Furthermore, after each professional learning session with Andrea, teachers will each name their own plans for what they will try in their teaching after each session. Still, the group makes an attempt at naming what they want to see teachers *doing* as a result of the professional learning by the end of the year:

- All teachers will post and students will independently access charts in the classrooms with key mathematical language and questions. These charts will change and build on each other across the year.

- All teachers will work with their grade-level colleagues to plan their daily lessons with a specific math goal in mind—this goal will be tied to standards and will be expressed throughout the lesson.

- All teachers will collaboratively plan complex tasks for students to solve, as frequently as appropriate in a unit of study, for students to talk about and solve together. These tasks will have multiple possible ways to work on solving them and will require students to argue mathematically.

- Students will talk about their thinking every day in math class.
- All teachers will listen to student discussions while they are solving these complex tasks and keep some sort of record of what they hear. More-experienced teachers will practice telling students what they are hearing and will practice sequencing student responses during the summary part of the lesson.

The leadership team knows that these implementation expectations will be challenging—but that they build on what the teachers are doing well—and are attainable if they worked together as a department.

They also decide that the teachers will select a subgroup of students to focus on during the professional development sessions and their grade-level teams this year. They will analyze these students' progress across the year. Rachel and Nadia emphasize the importance of selecting a group of students who are struggling and remind them of the school-wide focus on ELLs. The group wants the professional learning to help the teachers support their students who are struggling most in math, and they agree that this focus will give the implementation expectations even more significance.

## ARTICULATE THE SUPPORT PLAN

Reciprocal accountability means that we never ask teachers to do something without providing them sufficient support. The math leadership team considers what they think the teachers will really need in order to achieve the outcomes and expectations. This step is concerned with questions such as, What support will teachers need in order to be successful with implementation? How will I structure and communicate the support plan?

Sadie and Diane emphasize that the teachers will need help analyzing the curriculum, identifying priority standards, and preparing complex tasks. They think about how the department's collaboration time could be useful for some of this curricular work, but that when it comes to the task creation, they will need consultant support. They also discuss how the new teachers in the department especially will need help with classroom management as they take on the new tasks and that they feel they can provide this support to some extent during their coaching periods. They know that all teachers will struggle with letting go of control once they start encouraging more student talk and will need support with understanding that it will be OK!

Again, Rachel takes the role of listening, summarizing, and then stating what she hears. She agrees that indeed the team will need time to collaborate to understand the curriculum, they will need Andrea to help them design more-complex tasks and actually implement and learn from the implementation, and that the coaches will need to be able to support some of the teachers' management needs. She adds, "I am thinking that similar to last year, you will need to see what the new tasks will look like in the classroom—particularly how to facilitate the conversations. I think we'll probably be asking Andrea to provide more studio sessions again so you can see what the teaching and learning will look like, how to respond to student talk, and how to reflect on what happens." Diane and Sadie agree enthusiastically.

Rachel pauses and asks, indicating herself and assistant principal, Nadia, "What would be the most helpful roles for *us* from your perspective? What will the teachers need from us?"

Diane replies without hesitation. "We need your feedback and validation that we are trying something new and hard!" Sadie nods as Diane continues, "We are taking on some new practices that will push us. I know the teachers need to hear that this is important, that we are not also going to take on 10 other new things, and that our efforts are having an impact. And, when we say what we are going to try as a result of the PD—at the end of each session—please hold us to it—in a supportive way!" The two principals also nod and take a note about this need. They already have the practice of providing feedback, but they can tell they need to be even more strategic about when and how to provide it.

Rachel comments, "Of course, we will be there at the professional development when Andrea is here, and Nadia will be the one providing feedback in the classroom for math this year. Your comment makes me think about how we need to really prioritize that time for observing what you are trying on and providing feedback, particularly right after the professional learning has happened." She then asks them what they will need as teacher leaders in order to facilitate the PLC time and coach their peers effectively. Both teacher leaders comment that they will need time with Andrea to learn more about how to coach mathematics. They had started spending a bit of extra time with Andrea last year in order to prepare for their roles and know they have a lot more to learn. They hope that ultimately, perhaps in another year, they also may be ready to lead studio sessions themselves.

## IDENTIFY THE STRUCTURE AND RESOURCES FOR THE PD OPPORTUNITY

Rachel decides it is time to figure out the details, at least a rough draft to be revised as they learn more. The group steps back and looks at all of the learning support they have identified and agree on some next steps (the who, what, when, where, why).

First, they know they will prioritize the weekly department PLC time as an opportunity to work on unpacking the curriculum. They sense that over time, as they get better at designing and implementing complex tasks, they will also use PLC time to analyze student work from their shared tasks.

The team also agrees that they will carve out half of the eight days with the consultant this year to focus on Sadie and Diane—to support their coaching and facilitation of the department. They will have the remaining four days for the entire department to engage in studios and learn more about implementing complex math tasks. These visits have already been scheduled to occur roughly every other month for two days each. They also decide that Nadia, Sadie, and Diane will meet for 20 minutes weekly during first period on Mondays (one of their coaching periods) and visit classrooms together every other week to calibrate their observations and plan for the support and feedback. This will be a time for them to discuss what and how the team was learning. Sadie and Diane, they decide, will focus their daily coaching on the teachers in their first two years of teaching, at least for the start of the year. They even decide who will work with whom for the first coaching cycles.

The team feels this plan is reasonable and builds nicely off of the work of the previous year. They know that the addition of the weekly meetings for Nadia and the teacher leaders will help with keeping the math goals at the center of their discussions and thinking all year. They also are excited to think about the newer teachers getting additional support at the start of the year. The biggest change for the math department will be that the rest of the department will have only one day with the Andrea each time she visits. They will ultimately benefit because Sadie and Diane will be more prepared as a result of the time they are getting with Andrea. Rachel decides that she would craft an email to the department explaining the plan for the year, the rationale for the plan, the expectations and also include some language explaining her hopes for how the learning will evolve all year and benefit the students who needed the teachers the most.

The math leadership team is now prepared to embark on the year's learning together. Although the plan itself will require revision and development across the year, the fact that they are entering the year with some clarity about where they are going helps all the leaders in their roles. Having clear implementation expectations, for instance, will enable Diane and Sadie to follow up with teachers with precision. They will know what they are looking for and where they are going as coaches. The rest of the department will benefit from hearing the expectations and how they will be supported, and they will appreciate knowing that the plan is based on observational evidence as well as their ongoing input.

## DISCUSSION QUESTIONS

1. How does your leadership team determine professional learning goals now? To what extent and how do you develop specific goals with teacher and student expectations?

2. When and how do you engage others at your school in determining the needs and goals for the professional development? Who else could you include after reading about Mountain View's practices?

3. What are the resources and formal structures you currently have for professional learning? How are you coordinating those structures now?

## REFERENCE

The New Teacher Project. (2015). *The mirage: Confronting the hard truth about our quest for teacher development.* Brooklyn, NY: Author.

---

**Table 4.1**
**Planning for Focused Professional Learning**

Planning effective professional development requires many skills by instructional leaders. Leaders have to consider the context, identify the need, and structure the professional development so that the learning is clear and implemented effectively. Here are steps to consider as you plan professional development.

| STEPS | QUESTIONS TO ASK YOURSELF | OUTLINE AND RATIONALE |
|---|---|---|
| Consider the context. | What is the context of the professional development? Why is this context important? | There are many different contexts for professional development: new standards, new discipline-based pedagogy, teacher instructional needs, student learning needs, and district and school initiatives. It is important to identify the context in order to clearly identify the purpose for teacher learning. |
| Identify the need. | What are all of the things that teachers need right now? Which of those needs is the priority? **What are all of the aspects of the need (task analysis)?** What is the specific set of skills that teachers need right now to move their practice forward? | It is important to clearly identify why the professional learning is needed. If this is not done, the professional development will be unclear. Often, we identify needs too broadly: "Teachers don't plan." Instead, "Teachers don't have unit outcomes that can be clearly measured." |

*(continued)*

**Table 4.1**
(*continued*)

| STEPS | QUESTIONS TO ASK YOURSELF | OUTLINE AND RATIONALE |
|---|---|---|
| Articulate clear teacher and student outcomes. | Based on the identified need, write one or two outcomes for the professional development. Also, connect the teacher learning to student learning. *Teachers will understand or know _____ and that will result in students achieving _____.* | Once the need is identified, it is possible to identify clear teacher outcomes for the professional development. If possible, tie the teacher learning outcomes to student learning outcomes. We expect teachers to have clear outcomes for their lessons, and we need to have clear outcomes for professional development. Similar to how we consider the need, the outcomes should not be too broadly defined. They should be clear and measurable. |
| Articulate expectations for implementation. | Exactly what do I expect teachers to do based on this professional development? How will I know that they are doing it? | It is important to have clear expectations for the implementation. Teachers need to know exactly what they should be doing as a result of the professional development. |
| Articulate the support plan. | What support will teachers need in order to be successful with implementation? How will I structure and communicate the support plan? | Reciprocal accountability is essential when providing professional development. Essentially, if teachers are expected to implement, they need adequate support to do so (e.g., support from colleagues, coaches). |
| Identify the structure and resources for the professional development opportunity. | When should the learning happen? Who should lead it? Will it be more than one session? Which teachers should attend? | Once you know the need, the expectations, and the support that's required, you can consider how to structure the learning. This is the *who, what, where, when,* and *how* part of the planning. |

*Source:* © 2014 University of Washington Center for Educational Leadership.

**Table 4.2**

**Planning for Focused Professional Learning**

Math Department Professional Learning Plan

Mountain View Middle School

| STEPS | QUESTIONS TO ASK YOURSELF | MOUNTAIN VIEW'S THINKING |
|---|---|---|
| Consider the context. | What is the context of the professional development? Why is this context important? | • There is already a wide range of needs in the math classrooms, and this will become even more pronounced this year with integrating math classes.<br>• Teachers are not sure how to differentiate for all those students; most have fairly traditional preparation.<br>• There is a persistent gap in student scores, especially for ELLs.<br>• New textbooks this year will challenge all teachers.<br>• The math department continues to see turnover in teachers, and this year there are more novices and other teachers who are making decisions about if they want to remain in teaching.<br>• There is a school-wide focus on student engagement, particularly for ELLs.<br>• Teachers have begun to implement what they learned about supporting student talk.<br>• There is opportunity to build a collaborative, problem-solving culture to sustain and support all the teachers. |

(continued)

**Table 4.2**
*(continued)*

| STEPS | QUESTIONS TO ASK YOURSELF | MOUNTAIN VIEW'S THINKING |
|---|---|---|
| Identify the need. | What are all of the things that teachers need right now? Which of those needs is the priority? **What are all of the aspects of the need (task analysis)?** What is the specific set of skills that teachers need right now to move their practice forward? | • Teachers are having students talk more, making public records of student thinking, and ready to learn some ways to gather data from student talk and act on it.<br>• Most discussion tasks are procedural. The department is not sure how to create and implement other kinds of discussion opportunities.<br>• There is an opportunity to explore more reasons for student talk other than quick participation alone (e.g., meaning-making, grappling with complex problems, justifying thinking).<br>• Teachers requested support managing the curriculum and its pace.<br>• The consultant suggested there was a need for professional development on using the curriculum as a base for choosing or adapting complex tasks that require students to struggle and justify their thinking and then assess students' thinking as they talked. |
| Articulate clear teacher and student outcomes. | Write one or two outcomes based on the identified need for the professional development. Also, connect the teacher learning to student learning. *Teachers will understand or know _____ and that will result in students achieving _____* | • All math teachers will continue to learn structures and processes to develop and support mathematical discourse, to create anchor charts, and to create public records of student thinking, *which will result in* all students participating in written and verbal discussions that require them to argue mathematically and justify their thinking, particularly seventh-grade ELLs.<br>• All math teachers will learn to prioritize math goals and design correlating mathematical tasks that have multiple ways to solve them, *which will result in* all students (focus on seventh-grade students and ELLs) participating in discussions that require them to argue mathematically and justify their thinking. A measurable number of students will transfer these skills into their independent problem-solving.<br>• All math teachers will learn how to analyze student talk during these tasks, *which will result in* students understanding that they talk about math in order to explore, generalize, and develop justifications—not just to be "right." |

| | | |
|---|---|---|
| Articulate expectations for implementation. | Exactly what do I expect teachers to do based on this professional development? Which teachers? At what level? How will I know that they are doing it? | • All teachers will post and students will independently access charts in the classrooms with key mathematical language and questions. These charts will change and build on each other across the year.<br><br>• All teachers will work with their grade-level colleagues to plan their daily lessons with a specific math goal in mind—this goal will be tied to standards and will be expressed throughout the lesson.<br><br>• All teachers will collaboratively plan complex tasks for students to solve, as frequently as appropriate in a unit of study, for students to talk about and solve together. These tasks will have multiple possible ways to work on solving them and will require students to argue mathematically.<br><br>• Students will talk about their thinking every day in math class.<br><br>• All teachers will listen to student discussions while they are solving these complex tasks and keep some sort of record of what they hear. More-experienced teachers will practice telling students what they are hearing and will practice sequencing student responses during the summary part of the lesson. |
| Articulate the support plan. | What support will teachers need in order to be successful with implementation? How will I structure and communicate the support plan? | • Create time for the department to analyze the curriculum and prioritize standards during department planning time.<br><br>• Consultant support in helping with creating, implementing, and learning from complex tasks.<br><br>• Novice teachers will need classroom management support—probably from the coaches.<br><br>• All teachers will need to know from the leaders that it is OK to let go of control in the classroom when they start creating more opportunities for talk.<br><br>• Teachers will be given the opportunity to see the teaching and learning in place via studio sessions with the consultant.<br><br>• Teachers will need validation that they are trying something new, taking risks. Principals can provide this through feedback and their presence in sessions.<br><br>• Coaches will need more support from the consultant to learn how to coach. |

(continued)

**Table 4.2**
*(continued)*

| STEPS | QUESTIONS TO ASK YOURSELF | MOUNTAIN VIEW'S THINKING |
|---|---|---|
| Identify the structure and resources for the professional development opportunity. | When should the learning happen? Who should lead it? Will it be more than one session? Which teachers should attend? | • Provide department time for curriculum and standards analysis.<br>• Four of eight consultant days will focus on Sadie and Diane in their development as leaders.<br>• Four of eight consultant days will focus on time for the whole department to engage in studios to learn about—and practice implementing—the complex tasks and how students will engage in them.<br>• Leadership team will meet 20 minutes each Monday morning to visit classrooms and plan for support and feedback.<br>• Sadie and Diane will coach the new teachers during their release periods.<br>• Principal will send out an email to the math department summarizing the plan. |

# Table 4.3
## Planning for Focused Professional Learning

Literacy Professional Learning Plan

Mountain View Middle School

| STEPS | QUESTIONS TO ASK YOURSELF | MOUNTAIN VIEW'S THINKING |
|---|---|---|
| Consider the context. | What is the context of the professional development? Why is this context important? | • There is a wide range of reading and writing skill needs in the literacy classrooms. This year, all special education students are fully included in ELA for the first time, increasing the range of need in the classroom. |
| | | • Teachers are not sure how to differentiate for all those students; most have fairly traditional preparation—but they are interested in and asking questions about meeting more needs. |
| | | • Four of the six ELA teachers are in their first or second year of teaching. |
| | | • One of the teachers (Gary) has 17 years of experience in another school and has training in balanced literacy approaches. Gary has interest in becoming a teacher leader or coach and Rachel has found a way to fund one release period a day for him to coach his peers. |
| | | • The teachers do not have an official curriculum. Grade levels are responsible for developing their own curriculum based on standards. New teachers are finding they need additional time developing materials. |
| | | • There is a persistent gap in student reading and writing scores, especially for ELLs. |
| | | • There is a school-wide focus on student engagement, particularly for ELLs. |

(continued)

**Table 4.3**
*(continued)*

| STEPS | QUESTIONS TO ASK YOURSELF | MOUNTAIN VIEW'S THINKING |
|---|---|---|
| Identify the need. | What are all of the things that teachers need right now? Which of those needs is the priority? **What are all of the aspects of the need (task analysis)?** What is the specific set of skills that teachers need right now to move their practice forward? | • Because teachers have been trained fairly traditionally as secondary ELA teachers, they do not necessarily understand how to teach students *reading*. They are focused on assigning books even if students cannot access them on their own.<br>• 20% of students are reading two to three grade levels below their grade level and do not see themselves as readers—teachers are struggling with how to change this.<br>• The teachers value giving their students time to read their assigned texts but find it hard to fit in. They do not yet know how to match students to books that they can read. They tend to assume all students can just read the whole-class text. They also are not sure how to provide support to students so they can access the whole-class texts.<br>• Most classroom conversation is directed from student to teacher and back to student. The students do not yet have ways to talk to each other about their reading. |
| Articulate clear teacher and student outcomes. | Write one or two outcomes based on the identified need for the professional development. Also, connect the teacher learning to student learning. *Teachers will understand or know _____ and that _____ and that will result in students achieving _____.* | • Teachers will model how readers think and talk about themselves as readers, how they write about reading, how they overcome challenges as readers, how they challenge themselves as readers, problem-solve as readers authentically, make choices, and so on, which will result in the following:<br>• Students developing their identities and habits as readers as well as developing increasingly independent abilities to talk and write about texts as measured by the following:<br>• Purposeful reading surveys to assess reading identity and volume across the year (what to choose to read, why, how it is helping them grow and stay engaged) |

| | |
|---|---|
| | • Students coming to class regularly with the book they are reading every day, carrying the same book all day, talk about reading with each other informally, share books with each other<br><br>• Engaging in increasingly analytical conversations about reading during the year<br><br>• Teachers will understand and practice strategies for helping students know if they are reading a book at their level that will result in students completing at least one book a month with comprehension (as reflected in reading notebook entries and partner conversations). |
| Articulate expectations for implementation. | Exactly what do I expect teachers to do based on this professional development? Which teachers? At what level? How will I know that they are doing it? | • All ELA teachers will provide time (20 minutes) for students to read and write about books of their choice at their level every day.<br><br>• All ELA teachers will model their own thinking about reading and model their own writing about reading at least twice a week using a mini-lesson structure.<br><br>• All ELA teachers will provide and support student opportunities to talk about their reading with each other during independent reading at least twice a week (including support for ELLs).<br><br>• Some ELA teachers will confer with their students daily about their reading, rotating through the students according to a schedule they develop based on data. All ELA teachers will try out conferring at least once a week. |

(continued)

**Table 4.3**
*(continued)*

| STEPS | QUESTIONS TO ASK YOURSELF | MOUNTAIN VIEW'S THINKING |
|---|---|---|
| Articulate the support plan. | What support will teachers need in order to be successful with implementation? How will I structure and communicate the support plan? | • Create time for the department to discuss problems and successes as they open up time for students to read in class.<br>• Provide consultant support for modeling their thinking and conducting mini-lessons.<br>• Novice teachers will need classroom management support—probably from the coaches.<br>• Provide teachers with the opportunity to see independent reading with mini-lessons, conferring, and student talk during independent reading via studio sessions with the consultant.<br>• Teachers will need validation that they are trying something new, taking risks. Principals can provide this through feedback and their presence in sessions. Teachers will need reinforcement that independent reading is a good use of time in ELA.<br>• Coaches will need more support from the consultant to learn how to coach.<br>• Teachers will need to engage with professional texts about independent reading in middle school and learn more about young adult literature and how to tell if a student is comprehending—and what to do about it. |
| Identify the structure and resources for the professional development opportunity. | When should the learning happen? Who should lead it? Will it be more than one session? Which teachers should attend? | • Department time needs to be created to problem-solve, examine conferring notes, and discuss young adult literature.<br>• Four of eight consultant days will focus on Gary in his development as a leader.<br>• Four of eight consultant days will focus on time for the whole department to engage in studios to learn about—and practice implementing—independent reading with conferring and time for student talk.<br>• Leadership team will meet for 20 minutes each Monday morning to visit classrooms and plan for support and feedback.<br>• Gary will coach the new teachers during their release periods.<br>• The principal will send out an email to the literacy department summarizing the plan. |

*Source:* © 2014 University of Washington Center for Educational Leadership.

# Sponsoring Professional Learning

This chapter highlights how principals can take an active leadership role to sponsor teachers' professional learning. The example used here illustrates how the principal can be more strategic about what and how she communicates during a professional development (PD) session in ways that support teachers' implementation of what they learn. You will see the connections to the larger context of teacher learning at Mountain View Middle School and the formative classroom observations and careful planning that help to determine this specific PD opportunity. Indeed, part of what makes a principal's sponsorship of teachers' PD effective is the explicit connection to teachers' ongoing work and learning.

## THE IMPORTANCE OF SPONSORSHIP

With clarity about what the math department will learn this year and with specific ideas about how teachers' learning will be supported, Rachel now considers her own role *during* the PD sessions with the math consultant, Andrea. At CEL, we characterize this role as a sponsor for teachers' learning, and it is twofold. First, the sponsor signals interest and support. As a visible champion for teachers' learning, the leader's presence during the sessions with the consultant is an important demonstration of Rachel's commitment to the teachers'—and her own—learning. Second, being present is also an opportunity to learn more about what teachers are learning and to understand what might be difficult for teachers to implement. Understanding what makes the development of increasingly sophisticated teaching practice challenging will enable Rachel to work with teachers about the best way to move forward in their collective learning. If a principal knows teachers as learners and understands what makes the implementation of certain practices challenging, the principal can better support teachers' learning.

In a 2014 survey, teachers reported that the PD offered at their schools or districts was generally characterized by its fragmentation, lack of relevance to daily teaching, and lack of practical application to their core work of helping students learn (Bill & Melinda Gates Foundation, Author, Bill and Melinda Gates Foundation, 2014). A leader's sponsorship can help create coherence for PD and is a key consideration for instructional leadership.

A principal's role during a PD session is just as important as his or her role in planning for the session. No matter who is leading the PD—an outside consultant, a district leader or coach, or a school coach or teacher—the principal's sponsorship during the session is crucial for implementation. As a sponsor, the principal takes the lead in articulating the rationale for the PD session, connecting the dots between the current session and what teachers have been learning and working on, bringing forward compelling qualitative data about how students have been responding to what their teachers have been taking up in their practice, the questions raised by the teachers since the last session, and what the learning focus for the day will be.

Sponsorship not only takes places at the beginning of a session but also during and at the end of it as well. Table 5.1 (at the end of this chapter) summarizes the role of the leader as a sponsor for teachers' professional learning opportunities. This tool highlights key questions to help guide leaders as they open, participate in, and close the session. In what follows, we will highlight the use of this tool as Rachel thinks through her own sponsorship of a PD session with the math consultant, Andrea.

## OPENING A SESSION

A principal's message at the beginning of a session sets the tone for teacher learning, makes the purpose clear, and ties the learning to the big picture and the practicalities of daily teaching. If principals are not clear about what they want to say or the tone they want to communicate, they can unwittingly derail the opportunity for teacher learning. As previously mentioned, a principal's sponsorship is a way to frame the new learning within the larger context for teacher learning. Sponsorship can help teachers to connect their learning with practical ways to improve practice on behalf of their students.

Let's look at a *non*-example for a session opening:

Welcome! We are glad to have our math consultant back and I know we will learn a lot today, just as we do each time she visits. Just a reminder that the bathroom key is hanging just over there and that lunch break will be at 11:30. Please help yourselves to the coffee and donuts and let's have a great day of learning!

The purpose of the PD in this opening statement is not made clear, nor is it tied to a particular need teachers have. Teachers in this session would not know what to expect to learn, why it's important, nor how what they learn will help their students immediately or in the long term. Neither the teachers' nor the facilitator's role during the session is clear.

An ambiguous or vague opening to a professional learning session can unintentionally cause confusion, apathy, or reinforce ideas that leaders are out of touch with the realities of teachers' work with students and what makes sense for their learning. In fact, each occasion a principal has with her staff is an opportunity to continue to reinforce a vision for student learning and the power of teachers' practice to affect their students' learning. A leader's words matter—and as leaders listen to understand, summarize compelling ideas, and paraphrase collective learning, they can link essential messages about students' and teachers' capacities to the importance of the PD.

The intentional choice of language helps to introduce and reinforce a perspective of an ongoing, collective problem-solving orientation for continuous learning. If a school culture is defined by teachers working autonomously and in relative isolation of their colleagues, or if students are characterized as "low" or "high" kids, with more or less "readiness" to learn, then a principal's communication about continuous learning is even more important. By itself, rhetoric will not shift teachers' practice from isolated and idiosyncratic to collective, nor will words alone help teachers focus on their students' strengths and assets and shift a deficit orientation. But precise language that illustrates and reinforces the power of teaching to affect student learning, with specific reference to the challenges teachers face in their classrooms and how collective learning will enable us to rise to the challenges, sets a tone that recognizes the complexity of learning to teach well and the difference great teaching will make for students.

Now let's take a look at how Rachel opens this session, which is typical of her openings. As you read Rachel's opening, consider the guiding questions from the sponsoring professional learning tool and how Rachel's intentional framing, use of qualitative data about teaching practice and student learning, and explicit sponsorship set a clear tone of collective learning for the day:

Good morning, everyone! As always, I am excited for our day of working and learning together with our math consultant, Andrea. For the last year, we have been trying to figure out how to best address the gaps we see in the state math assessments for our English language learners. We have learned that getting students to actually talk about their thinking, take risks with how they communicate with one another, and use academic language to describe how they have come up with a solution and justify their answers is especially complex. But we know that learning how to help our students engage in math content in this way, developing their own thinking, and learning how to press each other is at the root of their performance issues. One thing we've learned together is that planning for robust and rigorous student discussion opportunities is a very sophisticated practice, requiring deep expertise of the math content you are teaching and deep knowledge of and appreciation for your students as individuals and as mathematicians. We have figured out how to have students talk about a procedure they have used, and we see that the entire department is asking students to report out their answers. We see that more students are talking in class and that students use the posted charts to support their conversations. But setting up tasks that are accessible for students *and* that require students to develop and communicate their thinking is our next step. And because we are adding a new textbook this year, we can leverage our learning time together to use this text to help us plan for the kind of mathematical tasks that support students' rich mathematical talk. As a team, we will continue to prioritize specific math goals based on standards and our students' needs, and now we have the curriculum materials as a base for choosing or adapting complex tasks that require students to justify their thinking. Today, we will continue to examine structures and processes to develop and support mathematical discourse, analyzing what is working well with the anchor charts and the public records of student thinking, how we will deepen our practice with these processes, and how to respond to student talk. We will dig into the new textbook as we design a task for a studio lesson that Andrea, Diane, and Sadie will try out together in Sadie's classroom during fourth period, with all of us focusing on particular students and their discourse during the lesson. As is always the case during these studio sessions, we all have the role of learning from one another and from the students' thinking. As we go through the course of the day, Andrea will take the lead facilitator role and my role is to learn alongside you. You will probably notice that I will ask clarifying or probing questions in the spirit of figuring out how to best support the team as we move forward. At the end of the day, together, we will agree on specific next steps we will take as the result of our learning. We want to be very clear about how the teaching practice we are getting better at will help our students and what, specifically, we can look for as evidence that students are indeed getting better. As an administrative team, we want clarity about what feedback will be most helpful and how best to work with you to keep the practice moving forward. I am going to turn this over to Andrea now . . .

## PARTICIPATION DURING THE SESSION

In this opening statement, note how Rachel sets a tone for the ongoing, collective learning for the work with the math consultant for the day and how the day's learning is tied to the larger context for teachers' learning; that is, this PD session is not an isolated event nor disconnected from the realities of teachers' continuous work. In addition to her opening remarks, Rachel's participation during the session was also intentionally planned. A principal can use the PD session to learn alongside teachers, which will help the principal to follow up with teachers, reinforcing and supporting new learning. Knowing enough about what teachers are taking up and trying in their practice makes a principal's feedback to teachers more helpful, linking their feedback with the support teachers have asked for. Principals can leverage their time in PD sessions as (1) an opportunity to learn more about the content and the complexity of teaching the content and (2) a means to inform subsequent classroom observations, leading to more-relevant individual feedback as well as formative data to inform teachers' collective learning.

### Learning and Leading Alongside Teachers

We often hear school leaders describe how they learn alongside teachers, deepening their knowledge of content, standards, and teaching practice. This learning helps leaders better understand what to observe and analyze when they are in classrooms and helps them deepen and extend the quality and boundaries of their own mental, conceptual maps of what "good" teaching looks and sounds like. Similar to teachers, leaders need to stay abreast of advances in teaching practices and the shifts in the learning demands placed on students as a result of rigorous content standards. Opportunities to participate as learners themselves enables principals to authentically engage alongside teachers as they develop together new understandings and an increasingly refined vision for the quality of student learning strived for, signaling the importance of such collective learning.

Principals' learning during a PD session with teachers not only grows their vision for teaching and learning but also shows how their subsequent leadership can support teachers' learning. Ensuring that PD is not a series of disconnected or isolated events requires leaders to think through how each opportunity with the consultant is based on actual needs of teachers and students and is part of the wider context of teachers' work. In the preceding chapters, we saw how Rachel closely plans with her leadership team and depends on teacher leaders to guide an overall learning plan based on the needs of students and teachers. Indeed, the PD session with a consultant is but one opportunity to learn, and for this opportunity to be maximized, it has to be woven into the larger tapestry for teacher learning at Mountain View Middle School or risk being seen as a top-down mandate, disconnected from the realities of teachers' classrooms and just another thing to do.

With this in mind, Rachel does more than sit in to learn during the sessions with the consultant. Rachel knows that she will learn more about teaching and learning mathematics. She will also be intentional about how to anticipate her subsequent support for teachers' learning. Rachel brings her understanding of students' needs and teachers' current practices to bear on her own participation. She is always aware of what her own participation and words signal and reinforce, knowing that she is always building and reinforcing a culture for teacher learning. Creating and sustaining a culture for teacher learning means that teachers have to be able to take risks with their practice and need coaching and feedback that enables them to engage in deliberate practice to develop new skills and habits of teaching. Rachel needs to be able to learn more about what teachers, as individuals, are learning in the session and figure out how best to support their learning in-between these sessions, linking her day-to-day leadership work to the development of teachers' practice on behalf of Mountain View students.

## The Leader's Focus

Prior to the session, Rachel decides that she needs to observe the math consultant, Andrea, as well as the participating teachers. Rachel wants to listen to the questions Andrea poses throughout the day and write down and categorize the questions the best she can. Are Andrea's questions meant to ascertain the teachers' understanding about student thinking, the math task itself, or how to scaffold a complex task? How is Andrea drawing out what teachers already know about their students or what barriers teachers perceive in their ability to try something new? How is Andrea assessing what teachers are confident with in their practice and what their biggest questions are? How do Andrea's questions spark reflection? Rachel anticipates that paying attention to Andrea's questions will help her elaborate her own learning about the finer points of teaching mathematics, as well as help her know more about the teachers as learners.

When observing the teachers, Rachel wants not only to pay attention to how the teachers respond to Andrea's questions but also to note any connection to the other structures and opportunities teachers have to learn from one another, for example, in department meetings, PLCs, or when Sadie and Diane are in classrooms. Rachel wants to watch for teachers' increasing ability to articulate their thinking and what support they ask for. Rachel wants teachers to do more than buy into professional learning; she wants agreement and ownership, collectively.

Prior to the session with the consultant, Rachel also thinks about when she might need to interject and the role she might play to guide teachers' learning. Because the consultant is not privy to the various conversations Rachel and the leadership team have had themselves, or with the other teachers, Rachel wants to listen for opportunities she might take to restate important ideas or prior agreements. In this case, Rachel wants to be able to reinforce ways to describe student learning, especially when they struggle, in ways that articulate what students *can* do and what they might be on the verge of doing, versus only noting what students are far from being able to do. She wants to articulate the same about teachers' practice, that is, what they are already doing and what they might be on the verge of doing. For example, the math department has already agreed to teach students to argue mathematically versus only getting a right answer to a problem. Such an agreement is at the core of Rachel being able to interject her thinking strategically; without prior, clear agreement about the focus for teachers' learning, how and why a leader would need to say anything during a PD session is, at best, ambiguous and, at worst, not at all helpful. Rachel also thinks about what she still needs to learn about the teachers' understanding, so paying attention to teachers' responses to the consultant's questions in order to learn more about the teachers as learners has to be balanced against her consideration as to when to interject.

Rachel also plans when she will actively participate as a learner, alongside teachers, and when she will prioritize her observation of teachers' learning. In this example, Rachel wants to have the same experience as the teachers when they begin to navigate the new textbook and design a task for students. Rachel knows she does not ultimately have to know what her teachers do about teaching mathematics, but she needs to know enough to be able to support teachers' subsequent learning. Rachel relies on her leadership team to guide her, but she has to be able to understand teachers' learning needs as well. This working knowledge allows Rachel to better understand how department meetings, the PLC, or other support structures might be leveraged for teachers' ongoing collective learning.

## CLOSING THE SESSION

Closing the session is another opportunity to reiterate expectations for implementation as well as the support teachers will receive to be successful at implementation. Throughout the session, Rachel has been paying attention to teachers' learning, thinking about how to be responsive to what teachers need. She is urgent about what the students at Mountain View Middle School need, day in and day out, in their math classes *and* she knows that teachers will need intentional practice to develop new skills. Rachel sees part of her role as a narrator for teacher learning, telling the story of teachers' ongoing learning journey and how this journey is ultimately about becoming better teachers on behalf of their students.

In order for Rachel's narration to be more than rhetoric, she is intentional about sharing specific evidence of teacher learning that she observes during the session. Throughout the session, Rachel pays attention to teachers' reflections, what they grapple with, how they articulate their own learning, and what kind of support they ask for. She wants to be able to highlight the ways in which the department talks with one another during the session—the questions they pose to each other, the way in which they offer up reflections and insights to a shared problem of teaching practice, and how their collective observations of student thinking during the studio session illustrates the growing expertise of the team. Rachel wants to celebrate this growth with teachers and wants to name the expertise that the math department continues to develop, highlighting what they are learning together. Linking the evidence of teacher learning to the PD session outcomes and naming how it links to what teachers are learning in their PLCs, department meetings, and with their colleagues' support in their own classrooms helps teachers see the various learning opportunities as connected and part of the broader context of their daily practice.

The session closing provides Rachel yet another occasion to narrate the learning journey the math department is on, articulating how the department started their learning journey, what they have figured out along the way, and what they now know they have to figure out next. This is another moment to articulate the rationale behind the learning teachers are engaged in—developing expertise so that teachers can get better at teaching Mountain View Middle School students. Rachel wants the team to be increasingly comfortable taking risks with their teaching practice so that they are poised to learn and deepen their skill sets. With this in mind, she takes every opportunity to name what teachers are already doing in their practice and what they will need support with. In this session, for example, Rachel notes that the process of designing tasks together and using the new textbook will require additional practice before teachers can make such planning a habit. She wants to name for teachers what help to expect from Sadie and Diane during department meetings and PLCs that would support them to hone this new habit of planning.

At the close of each PD session with the consultant, Rachel asks all teachers to name what they will try out as a result of their learning and what support they need from the leadership team. She listens for the connections to the teachers' year-long professional learning goal, wanting to be clear about how each teacher's individual request for support also fits with collective longer-term capacity-building goals.

Let's look at how Rachel closes the day:

Thank you everyone for your participation and learning today. I want to especially thank Andrea for your facilitation and expertise—and also Sadie for opening your classroom for our studio lesson. Make sure you extend our thanks to your students as well for opening their mathematical thinking and risk-taking for all of our learning. I am leaving today thinking in particular about Edgar, one of Sadie's ELL students whom many of us know. I have watched a transformation in him this year in math. He came to us late in the year last year and he used to barely make it to math class, and when he did make it, he would sit in the back with his head down. Now, look at him. Today I heard him say to his partner and then to the whole class, after Sadie's encouragement and language support, "I understand that we have three different ways to solve this problem right now. If all three of these methods work, what does that mean? What is the pattern here?" Let's keep collecting examples like this of students developing more confidence and academic language skills. And, I am excited for all of us to continue to reflect, as you did all day, on what we do as teachers to make moments like this possible. For instance, today I heard a lot of positive buzz after the studio lesson. I heard you sharing examples of student discourse with each other and I noted something that Samantha said that I want us to all hear again. She said, "OK, it really was worth it to slow down and create the task together while thinking through all the possible misconceptions and how to respond if they come up. I don't usually do that, but I can see the benefit. We were able to make better guesses about the kinds of support the kids would need in their language as well as in the math." I see many of you nodding right now. This was also probably my biggest learning today as well, so thank you, Samantha, for saying it! I will continue to encourage you to slow down like this as much as you can. You know your students better than you did last year; we have all acknowledged that. You have better information about what the students can do because of the tasks you are creating together—so you can truly plan with the standards and the students in mind. That was so powerful to see today. You have Sadie and Diane to lead that work in the PLCs. You have them available for some coaching. You have Nadia and me available to observe you and cheer you on with some formative feedback. I am going to give you some time to reflect. Think about the students in your focus group—your ELL students. Get specific. What do you want to hear them saying by the end of the year as they work on these tasks? Ask yourself, what will you do next to support them? And, what support do you need from the leadership team? I am eager to hear these thoughts and excited for your students.

## CONNECTING LEARNING AND IMPLEMENTATION

Although careful planning for a PD session helps leaders be explicit about what teachers will learn and what they will be able to do as a result, reinforcing and signaling expectations about what, exactly, will be implemented gives leaders and teachers clarity about what it will look and sound like as teachers begin to implement new practices. Such clarity reinforces prior agreements about the learning for the year and provides further definition for leaders' classroom observations. As leaders learn alongside teachers, gaining better understanding of what it might look like as teachers try out new practices and how students will respond, leaders are better equipped to problem-solve *with* teachers.

In Chapter 6 we will see how Rachel and the leadership team plan to follow up on the learning of the PD session, taking into account the teachers' requests for support. You will see the specific and strategic plan that the leadership team develops and how this plan builds on the learning of the discrete PD session, year-long goals, and specific teachers' needs.

## DISCUSSION QUESTIONS

1. What role do you currently play during teachers' professional development?

2. How do you currently leverage the expertise of consultants who work with teachers in your building?

3. What aspect of teacher learning or culture building might you take a more active role to sponsor? Why?

## REFERENCE

Bill & Melinda Gates Foundation. (2014). *Teachers know best: Teachers' views on professional development*. Seattle, WA: Author.

### Table 5.1
### Sponsoring professional learning: A principal's role

A principal's role during a professional development session is just as important as his or her role in setting the larger context or planning for the session. No matter who is leading the professional development—an outside consultant, a district leader or coach, or a school coach or teacher—the principal's sponsorship during the session is crucial for implementation.

| STEPS | QUESTIONS TO ASK YOURSELF | OUTLINE AND RATIONALE |
|---|---|---|
| Open the session. | • What is the purpose of the professional development?<br>• How does the purpose tie to a need?<br>• What exactly will teachers learn today and why is that important?<br>• How will what they learn help their students immediately or in the long term?<br>• What is the teacher's role today?<br>• What is the facilitator's role? | A principal's message at the beginning of a session sets the tone for teacher learning, makes the purpose clear, and ties the learning to the big picture and the practicalities of daily teaching. If principals are not clear about what they want to say or the tone they want to communicate, they can unwittingly derail the opportunity for teacher learning. |

*(continued)*

**Table 5.1**
*(continued)*

| STEPS | QUESTIONS TO ASK YOURSELF | OUTLINE AND RATIONALE |
|---|---|---|
| Participate during the session. | • What do I want to observe in the facilitator's work and what do I want to observe in the teacher's learning? Why?<br><br>• When will I interject and guide teacher learning? When will I let the teacher learning take its course?<br><br>• When will I actively participate in the learning?<br><br>• How will I help teachers connect their learning to the expectations for implementation? How will I signal this during the session? | A principal's participation during the session can signal the importance of teacher learning. If no one is present or supporting the learning or making it clear, teachers will see the session as just another thing to do or another unclear and disconnected initiative or session. It's important to value teacher learning as an instructional leader. It's not enough to just sit in. The principal's role during the session is planned intentionally. |
| Close the session. | • What evidence of teacher learning is important to highlight?<br><br>• How did the evidence of teacher learning meet the outcomes of the session?<br><br>• What did I see during the session that showed me that the teachers will be successful during implementation?<br><br>• What did I see during the session that showed me that teachers will need more support? What kind of support? What is the plan for supporting teachers?<br><br>• What specific link do I want to make to their work the next day? | Closing the session is an important way to bridge teacher learning to implementation. The closing provides an opportunity to share evidence of teacher learning during the session. It's also a time to reiterate expectations of implementation and the support teachers will receive to be successful at implementation. |

*Source:* © 2014 University of Washington Center for Educational Leadership.

# A Process for Following Up

## chapter SIX

This chapter will explore the complexities of leaders planning for strategic follow-up after a professional learning opportunity or series of opportunities. Intentional and strategic follow-up is perhaps even more crucial than the initial planning for the professional learning opportunity, especially when we consider what is required to support implementation. Mountain View Middle School approaches the task of planning this follow-up as a collaborative effort, not the sole responsibility of one leader or the diffuse responsibility of all the individual teachers or leaders on their own. We believe that intentional follow-up is not about heavy-handed accountability or checking for compliance; rather, leaders consider what teachers are understanding and approximating in their practices and also whether the professional learning is having the desired effect on student learning. They ask to what extent they have evidence that teachers are working together to collaboratively solve problems of student learning. In order to successfully plan for follow-up, the leadership team at Mountain View reviews student data and classroom observation data, examines department goals, studies the consultant's report, considers individual teacher's goals, and plans for next steps using their support structures—feedback, coaching, and teaming.

One Monday morning in early December, the members of the Mountain View math leadership team gather in Nadia's office for their weekly meeting. Sadie and Diane have a stack of student papers in front of them from their own students and from the students of the two new teachers they have been most intensively coaching, Samantha and Bob. Nadia and Rachel have their notes and the consultant report from the most recent professional development session with Andrea. Rachel welcomes the team and frames the purpose. "We just had some powerful professional learning with Andrea last week, I know you just administered an important assessment, and we have four weeks until winter break. Our task is to think through what we need to do to really follow up and ensure we are moving forward as a math department on behalf of our students—particularly the ELLs we identified this fall. How should we do this today?" Rachel asks the group.

Sadie and Diane start talking over each other with excitement. "We are finally starting to see some growth in our focus group ELL students!" Diane shares, displaying her students' work on a mathematical task the seventh-grade teachers have piloted. "These four boys started the year in our classes with big gaps in their computation and algebraic understanding. When Andrea was here in November, we worked on an open-ended task that would measure the standard—which had lots of ways to enter the problem. It really helped to keep the students in productive struggle longer than I would have on my own. They were into the problem and even though it was hard, I let them struggle." The group nods. "And after a few days of work in groups with our support, look at what these boys can do now!" The group looks over the students' work and comments that that they all see progress. Sadie mentions that she has had similar success with her students, particularly given the support she creates for them to ask for help. "These samples here, however, are from the other classes. We all analyzed our student work on this task in our PLC last week. Samantha and Bob did not see growth in their focus students. They were really discouraged, and we are now worried they will start to revert back to how they were teaching before. They said as much . . ." Sadie holds a chart in front of her summarizing the results of the assessment for *all* focus group students from all the teachers in the department. As they study the data for a few minutes, the group agrees that the other teachers' results have shown more student progress as a whole. Although this is not always the case, the data suggest that the teachers who have been trying out the new practices see almost immediate change in student learning.

Rachel comments, "That is interesting. The teachers were so positive after the studio session—there was a lot of energy and interest in trying new things! And, our classroom observations show that teachers are trying out new ways to engage students with complex tasks and give them the chance to talk about their reasoning. These student results must be discouraging to Samantha and Bob. We can use some of our time today to plan for some next steps with them specifically—remember, they are newer teachers. Let's go back to everyone's goals and think about what your role with each teacher might be and what role Nadia or I should play. I think it would help us all to also look over the notes Andrea sent after our professional learning studio last week and review the big picture."

The group agrees that this makes sense. They spend about 10 minutes reviewing and discussing Andrea's notes from the previous session. Andrea has made several general notes about the department as a whole, including advice for the teachers in their planning and implementation. Her notes include specific observations about the thinking the teachers are ready to keep doing as they plan for and implement mathematical tasks:

- Teachers, continue to focus on the math goal for each lesson when planning tasks (What do you want students to understand at the end of today's lesson? How will this task measure that goal? Does this task have sufficient entry points for all the students?)

- Teachers, continue to focus on formative assessment while implementing the new tasks (How will you know if they understand the math goal?)

- Coaches, ask teachers what the cognitive demands of the tasks are.

- Principals, when you observe, pay attention to

  - Students working together to solve a complex problem that takes a few days, generally divided into three parts. The problem should require mathematical explanation and argument, not just a procedure.

  - Teachers circulating, taking notes, and supporting students as needed, asking some students to share their thinking with the whole class, supported with sentence frames as needed.

  - In the next few weeks, increasing amounts of student talk in small groups about math tasks that require them to reason.

  - Individual teachers' next steps as named in final reflection notes.

She also made specific recommendations for Samantha and Bob:

- Bob may need support with a reset of expectations with his students. Management of routines, particularly for discussion and work completion, seems to be hindering what he can accomplish. He will also need help anticipating where students will struggle so he can plan appropriate tasks with appropriate support.

- Samantha needs intensive support on planning for complex tasks. She is interested in this work and she is asking for this support from her colleagues. In the classroom, she is trying out new structures to support student talk—these will need reinforcement because it is so new to her.

Nadia has already sketched out her feedback cycles for the month knowing that she needs to spend additional time with these newer teachers. She has a sense of their goals for the year and what they want to try after the last PD, but she knows that the more specific she can be with her feedback, the better. She also knows that the intensive support on math content and lesson planning has to come from Diane and Sadie. The school has structures in place to support the teachers, but the math leadership team knows they have to be clearer about the purpose of each. Nadia also realizes that she has to be flexible—she cannot map out her feedback cycles all at once and assume they will go as planned. She allows for the space to adjust her plans based on what they are all learning.

Next, they remind themselves about the department's year-long outcomes:

- All math teachers will continue to learn structures and processes to develop and support mathematical discourse, to create anchor charts, and to create public records of student thinking, *which will result in* all students participating in written and verbal discussions that require them to argue mathematically and justify their thinking, particularly seventh-grade ELLs.

- All math teachers will learn to prioritize math goals and design correlating mathematical tasks that have multiple ways to solve them, *which will result in* all students (focus on seventh-grade students and ELLs) participating in discussions that require them to argue mathematically and justify their thinking. A measurable number of students will transfer these skills into their independent problem-solving.

- All math teachers will learn how to analyze student talk during these tasks, *which will result in* students understanding that they talk in math in order to explore, generalize, and develop justifications—not to just be "right."

They also review the goals Samantha and Bob had set at the start of the school year and during the previous week after the professional development session with Andrea.

| GOAL | SAMANTHA | BOB |
|------|----------|-----|
| Year-long professional goal | Co-create anchor charts with students to support their talk in every unit and develop structures (such as A-B partners) for students to work together as they talk while engaging in mathematical tasks, which will result in students being able to explain their thinking using math language and ELL students increasing performance on their unit assessments. | Set up and reinforce classroom routines that allow students to talk to each other productively, share their ideas with the whole class, and access materials they will need for problem-solving during complex mathematical tasks, which will result in all students engaging in productive academic talk most of the time and target ELL students justifying their thinking verbally and in writing. |
| Their stated short-term goals at the end of the most recent professional learning session *and* **response to the question, What support do you need?** | Try out an anchor chart that will help students with the math goal and direct them to the chart when they are confused so I don't have to be the one answering all the questions. **I need feedback on this to know if I am on the right track.**<br><br>When I create mathematical tasks, make sure they enable students to grapple with complex mathematical thinking. **I need help with planning—Diane? Sadie? PLC?** | Allow more time for students to share their answers with the whole class. Set these opportunities up so that students can share using mathematical language that the other students can listen to. **Coaching? Feedback?** |

"OK," Nadia begins, "I am beginning to see some direction for the next four weeks before we go on break, and then we can pick up the plan again after the holidays—really until the end of the semester in January." Given the overall department goals, the student math assessment results, Andrea's notes, and the teachers' individual goals, Nadia sees even more reason to prioritize Samantha and Bob. "Bob is brand-new this year and Samantha is in her second year of teaching, and we have seen growth from year one. We want that to continue," Nadia comments.

"How should we do this?" Rachel asks. "We want to remember the needs of the math department as a whole, and we want to make sure we have some clear reasoning, goals, and expectations if we are going to be focusing on two people intensively."

Sadie and Diane remind the team that department PLC time each week would provide support to all teachers as they plan for instruction. "It seems Andrea's main recommendation for the department is to keep our focus on these questions: What is the math goal? How will this task measure this goal? How do we ensure multiple entry points? How will we know if they understand? We can do that. Andrea has helped us by modeling a process for considering student assessment data, prioritizing standards, and then selecting lesson materials—we can replicate that process in the PLC." They know that between the two of them, they can take leadership for supporting planning in all grades (6, 7, 8) because they both taught seventh grade. Sadie can take the lead for sixth and Diane can take the lead for eighth. Nadia comments that she will still visit each math classroom at least once a week, even for just 10 minutes. "I can reinforce your work by asking teachers to share with me their math goal for the lesson and then I can listen to students so I can hear how the task lets them grapple with that goal."

"Do we think that PLC planning time will be enough for Samantha and Bob to really take this work on?" Diane asks. The group agrees that these teachers will need more than the collaborative time—which will help with content planning but not instruction. Rachel recommends that Diane and Sadie continue to work with Samantha and Bob during their coaching time because they are both newer, had some specific short-term requests, and are at a point in their teaching at which they could slide back into their default practices (showing students how to solve the problems, doing more of the thinking than the students, over-scaffolding, providing limited time for students to talk). Based on the recommendations from Andrea for a classroom routine reset and given Bob's request to set up more opportunities for student whole-group sharing and Diane's strong relationship with him, the group agrees that Diane will continue coaching Bob on his classroom routines. "I can imagine sitting down with Bob and planning out how to teach clearer expectations for the whole class period—bell to bell—with a particular focus on how to structure student share time and how to teach students to listen and respond to other students sharing." Everyone nods and Rachel takes some notes. Diane continues, "I am also excited to try out coaching him side-by-side in the classroom, which is something Andrea and I practiced during her visit. I can help him with the entire process. I bet we could determine some specific goals for his practice and his students' participation during these routines—and then assess his progress—and theirs—after a few weeks."

Nadia asks Diane what her role as the assistant principal should be. "I think it would be best if I get a few weeks to work with him and then maybe you go in and give feedback. I think he will need time to practice," Diane replies.

Nadia nods. "OK, but let me know if I can help with the reset. I will plan to stay in touch with you about it and of course will try to get in there once a week. Maybe at the beginning of January it would make sense for me to provide some targeted feedback based on what you worked on in coaching. With Bob—I worry about him letting the practices go when things get hard." The group agrees that this makes sense.

Sadie says, "OK, what about Samantha? She is very clear that she wants some feedback on her use of anchor charts and her efforts to get students to be more independent when they are working. I agree that is a solid goal for her—and it's huge that she wants to try it out right away." Nadia and Rachel whole-heartedly agree. Nadia decides that she will follow up immediately with Samantha and find out more about the nature of the feedback she wants. (We will describe the feedback cycle with Samantha in more detail further on in this chapter.) "What about the other part of her goal, though?" Sadie asks. "And Andrea's recommendation that we really support her with planning mathematical tasks?"

Nadia and Rachel nod, and Nadia comments, "Sadie, I think you are going to be the right person to keep coaching her about her planning and implementing of tasks. She's been involved in the department learning all year and this planning work continues to challenge her. She would really benefit from more time with you to get those tasks really planned well. What do you think is in the way?"

Sadie thinks about this and then comments, "This is new and hard work for all of us. I think Samantha in particular is so new to all the standards of mathematical practice that she thinks her students need all of it—prioritizing is a struggle for her. In her first year, she worked mostly on her management, so it's only recently that she has been able to really pay attention to content in a significant way. She also has a few beliefs about students that worry me a little. I still think she sees the students as blank slates with limited background." The group has been grappling with how to address beliefs such as Samantha's and has no ready answer. "I think focusing on what she is teaching can help her get clearer about assessing what the students are able to do—which will help with prioritizing goals. I think I need to work with her on planning tasks and on how to listen to students while they are working collaboratively. I want to point out what they *can* do." The group finds this solution workable. Rachel wonders aloud if having Sadie's coaching and Nadia's feedback at the same time would be overwhelming. "Let's ask her. My guess is that as long as we are working on similar things, I think it will be OK. We could propose that we stagger it—maybe coaching first for a few weeks and then feedback. I think my feedback on her anchor chart work is really tied to your work on tasks and assessment." Sadie agrees. "We need to ensure she sees it that way."

The group sums up the plan for the next four weeks and first two weeks after winter vacation. They recognize that to arrive at this plan, they have to ask themselves these questions, based on data and reflections: What kind of support does every teacher need? Why? How will that support be provided? What do some teachers need? How will that support be best provided? What additional information do we need?

| SUPPORT FOR ALL MATH TEACHERS | SUPPORT FOR SAMANTHA | SUPPORT FOR BOB |
|---|---|---|
| • Provide weekly PLC collaboration focused on planning tasks and analyzing student progress. Sadie and Diane facilitate.<br><br>• Nadia will observe each classroom informally at least once a week asking herself and the teacher (before or after the observation), What is the math goal today? and Nadia will share her notes on what students are saying and doing during the opportunities to talk about the complex tasks.<br><br>• Take weekly calibration walks with the whole math leadership team to formatively analyze what is in place (two to three classrooms per week). | • Three weeks of daily classroom coaching (one period a day) with Sadie including at least two whole planning periods a week to design tasks and look at student work. Daily classroom coaching (side-by-side) on listening to students, directing them to the anchor charts, and using the information to plan for the next tasks. To measure progress, Sadie and Samantha will closely examine ELL student work during class and during their biweekly planning.<br><br>• Two-week feedback cycle with Nadia focusing on student independent use of anchor charts, possibly after the coaching. Nadia will ask Samantha to clarify the exact feedback focus and timing of the feedback. | • Four weeks of daily coaching with Diane (one to two periods a day) to plan and implement a reset of expectations and develop a process for students to share and listen to each other. Bob and Diane will plan look-fors to measure how students are growing.<br><br>• Nadia will provide targeted feedback to Bob in early January focused on his classroom routines, particularly for students sharing their thinking with the whole class. |

After the six-week period has come to an end, the math leadership team will again spend their weekly meeting reviewing student and teacher data in order to prepare for a call with Andrea to plan the upcoming math studio in mid-February. They will ask themselves these questions: What are we seeing in student progress on these math tasks and their engagement in the class? What are we seeing in teacher practice with respect to their goals? What are teachers saying now? What are we all learning about the support that is needed? This degree of close examination of classroom practice accompanied by support—as requested by the teachers—will ensure that the team maintains an improvement focus as the year progresses.

## WRAPPING UP THE MEETING

Looking back across their follow-up plan, including the targeted feedback, coaching, and PLC, the math team at Mountain View feels prepared to focus the department's energy for the remaining six weeks of the semester. They also recognize the need to stay flexible and make course corrections along the way as needed—as determined through their formative observations of practice, their conversations with teachers, and the results of student assessments that PLCs analyze together each week. They review, once again, the goals the teachers have set and the goals for the department as a whole so they are clear about what they will be looking for as evidence of progress.

## A CLOSER LOOK AT TARGETED FEEDBACK: ONE TOOL FOR LEADERS

We mentioned previously in this chapter that Nadia intends to engage in cycles of targeted feedback with Samantha and Bob. In each case, the teachers are implementing new learning and are trying on new instructional practices. We find that targeted feedback is a helpful strategy for a leader to use to follow up on teacher learning when there is a practice that the teacher is very close to being able to implement. We find that by providing feedback based on these incremental changes in practice, within a teacher's goal and within that teacher's zone of proximal development, leaders can ensure that new practices take hold and ultimately have the greatest effect on students.

There are lots of ways to provide feedback. Targeted feedback is a way to provide actionable, evidence-based, growth-oriented feedback tied to the teacher's goal. It can be a way to reinforce a practice that is not yet solid. We know from research on improvement that we do not necessarily get "better" at a skill by practicing it on our own hour after hour. We need a particular type of practice—deliberate practice or practice with guidance and feedback—to master a new skill (Ericsson & Pool, 2016).

We have found that teachers progress quickly with frequent feedback, tailored to their questions and captured in brief observations with brief conversations. Leaders often want to provide this timely, specific, actionable feedback but struggle with fitting it into their schedules. Nadia and the team at Mountain View Middle School have been experimenting with a process for feedback that includes three main types of conversation: *planning conversation, affirmation or next step conversation,* and *reflection conversation* (see Tables 6.1 through 6.4 at the end of this chapter). Each conversation enables a principal to prepare to observe in a focused way and then provides very specific follow-up feedback. Each conversation has a rough structure that enables the principal to remain purposeful and time-efficient. After the initial planning conversation, the conversations and observations are no more than 5 to 15 minutes each—because they are so focused. When Nadia comments she needs more information about the nature of the feedback Samantha wants, she is already thinking about having a planning conversation to confirm the focus and plan for the specific observation process. After the planning conversation, Nadia will have enough information to plan for a set of short, focused observations and feedback conversations—and then ultimately a reflection conversation. Note that Nadia first checks in with Samantha about the timing of the feedback cycle and Samantha agrees that waiting until three weeks of coaching are over is a good idea. At that point, she will have more complex tasks in place and will need support in sustaining this practice.

What follows in this chapter are examples of scripts from two conversations between Nadia and Samantha. Tables 6.1 through 6.4 at the end of the chapter include the general structures for these conversations. You might want to reference them to note the architecture for each conversation as you read through the following scripts.

## Planning Conversation

*Nadia:* Thanks for your willingness to meet today. I am looking forward to supporting you with your goal. By the end of this conversation, I hope we will have a specific focus for my feedback cycle with you and clear indicators of success so we can measure along the way and at the end.

*Samantha:* Sounds great.

*Nadia:* Your goal for the year is to work on creating structures for student talk during mathematical tasks, including creating anchor charts with students that will help students as they work in groups. I know that after the last professional development session with Andrea, you also said that you want to work on anchor charts that will keep students working while they are grappling with complex tasks. You've had some coaching since that last PD, so I want to make sure that this is still the focus you want. Things can change.

*Samantha*: Yes. I still really struggle when students are working on their own or in groups and they all want my help at once. Sadie helped me a lot with planning tasks and setting them up. When the two of us are in there and she is circulating with me to point out what the students are doing well, I am fine. I am worried a little that on my own I will be less positive and patient.

*Nadia*: What have you been learning so far about how to support students' independence while they are struggling?

*Samantha*: Well, I know that when I make the tasks more complex, which Sadie and my department team are helping me do, the students start out more engaged but then they get frustrated and some of them shut down and stop working. I have to run around and try to help all of them at once get unstuck. Sadie did help me see that not everyone shuts down, and she gave me some strategies for having students share their thinking in their groups, but it's slow.

*Nadia*: What have you tried?

*Samantha*: The biggest thing we tried was setting up some charts in the room. One chart describes what to do when you are mathematically stuck. The kids helped create the chart so it's in their words. I also have charts up with important vocabulary and some of the problem-solving strategies we have learned. This works sometimes; some students reference them and keep working. When I get overwhelmed, though, I just start running around and helping them individually instead of letting them figure things out.

*Nadia*: What kind of support would you like from me?

*Samantha*: If you come in and see students working on their own in their groups, referencing the charts, will you tell me? I need to remember that some are doing that. Also, will you tell me when you see I resist running around and "helping"? Sadie thinks that will work, but I am not always convinced.

*Nadia*: OK, so I will observe for evidence of students figuring things out on their own, not asking you for help. I will also observe for instances when you step back and remind students of their resources—and see what the effect of that is.

*Samantha*: That will be great. It's hard to change how I typically work and I want them to be successful.

*Nadia*: Of course. What should we look for after these two weeks that would show progress for you and for the students?

*Samantha*: I think that it would be huge if we saw in your scripts that I decrease in the amount I tell students how to approach problems when they are struggling and increase in the amount of times I just point to a chart as a reminder and then walk away. It would be huge if we saw the students looking at the charts without me pointing at them by the end of the cycle! What if we saw no students raise their hands to ask me to rescue them? I'd love to see them work first with each other, then check a chart, then maybe ask another group. I'd love to see this for my focus students in particular.

*Nadia*: Great! I can do that. And, I can focus on your ELL students. Based on these outcomes, when should I first come in and then how often?

*Samantha*: Well, we are starting set standard character, not a swash character new task on Friday. The first day is when I really want to help them the most. Why don't you come in Friday, sixth period, and then if we focus on sixth period for the whole cycle . . . that would help. There are a number of students in that period who really want my help all the time. You and I could then debrief quickly right after school.

*Nadia*: That works. Why don't I come in and observe sixth period every other day for a while—maybe until break? So, two weeks, starting this Friday? And we can try to debrief right after school at 3 pm, no more than five minutes so I can go supervise the buses.

*Samantha*: That would be perfect.

*Nadia*: OK, see you Friday!

On Friday, Nadia observes Samantha's sixth-period class during the 15 minutes when students were grappling with the complex task for the first time. She gathers data on students' use of the charts and Samantha's responses to students to keep them working. Nadia takes 10 minutes out of the class while Samantha is wrapping up in order to plan her next step feedback conversation. She returns to the classroom just as the students start filing out of the portable classroom behind the main building.

## Next Step Conversation

*Nadia*: I so appreciate your openness to this feedback cycle. It is a tremendous help to your students to see you work this way! As you know, the purpose of this conversation is to give you some feedback on your students' independence as they were working today and your actions that supported that independence, particularly for your ELLs.

*Samantha*: That's great. I am curious what you saw.

*Nadia*: I noticed the following things that relate to that focus. First, when you handed out the tasks to the groups, you pointed to the three main charts on the front of the room—one with the getting unstuck tips, one with vocabulary, and one with the problem-solving reminders. That resulted in Jorge's group—the group with Jorge, Belinda, and Marcus—looking up at the vocabulary chart and using it to help them discuss what the task actually said. Jorge in particular took the lead on looking at the chart and telling his group to look at it, too.

*Samantha*: I am glad to hear that!

*Nadia*: Then, when the students really got working, I noticed you went over to Jorge's group and it looked like you were going to maybe give them a little help, but then you literally took a step back and just watched them and then walked away. In the next few minutes, they pointed to the problem-solving chart on their own five times—and got started working with a set of manipulatives from the cabinet.

*Samantha*: It was really hard for me to do that. I wouldn't have suggested manipulatives, so it was good that I didn't make *my* suggestion. Their choice to use manipulatives will help them in the end. Thanks; it helps to hear that they did that. I noticed that when I tried not to swoop in and save the other groups, too, today, they actually worked on their own longer than I thought.

*Nadia*: What will you try next?

*Samantha*: Well, Monday is when they have even more time to work on the next part of the problem, and then they have the final part of the problem Tuesday. I will keep practicing pointing out the charts at the start of the explore phase and then practice stepping back when I think they need me in the groups. I am not sure what to do though when they start to lose stamina as they have more time to struggle. If I interrupt class to point out the chart to the whole class I might interrupt the flow that some students may have.

*Nadia*: OK, what if you try pointing out a chart to one of the students who is struggling and encourage that student to tell the others to use it?

*Samantha*: I can try that.

*Nadia*: Great. I will see you Tuesday, and I will watch the students working and your responses to them with pointing to the charts. Thanks!

## DISCUSSION QUESTIONS

1. How do you typically follow up on teacher professional learning? How do you elicit what support teachers need?

2. After professional learning has occurred, how do you determine what to look for in the classrooms?

3. What role do you play when external providers come in and provide professional development? How do you set up the work? What do you ask providers to share after the sessions?

# REFERENCES

Ericsson, K. A., & Pool, R. (2016). *Peak: Secrets from the new science of expertise*. New York, NY: Houghton Mifflin Harcourt.

Marzano, R. J., Frontier, T., & Livingston, D. (2011). *Effective supervision: Supporting the art and science of teaching*. Alexandria, VA: Association for Supervision and Curriculum Development.

## Table 6.1
## Planning conversation

Conversations with a teacher are situated within a cycle of teacher learning. Therefore, there are multiple types of conversations. The purpose of the planning conversation is to review the teacher's area of focus and decide on the outcomes, the number of observations, and the types of conversations for the targeted feedback cycle.

- The *primary* purpose of ongoing classroom observations is not to judge the quality of teachers but to find the most effective way to support teachers' growth.
- Frequent observation leads to *less,* not more, apprehension (Marzano, Frontier, & Livingston, 2011).

| STEPS | POSSIBLE QUESTIONS, STEMS OR FRAMES | OUTLINE AND RATIONALE |
|---|---|---|
| Set the context, if needed. | • As you know, the way I'm observing and giving feedback is changing.<br>• The purpose of this conversation is to …<br>• By the end of the conversation, I hope we will … | Setting the context for targeted observation and feedback helps to make the purpose of this planning conversation transparent. |
| Share the district and school goals (based in the instructional framework). | • As a school, we're working on …<br>• Your area of focus is …<br>• Here's how it sits within the instructional framework …<br>• How do you see the connection? | Creating coherence among the school goals, district goals, and the instructional framework situates the teacher's area of focus within a larger context. |

*(continued)*

## Table 6.1

*(continued)*

| STEPS | POSSIBLE QUESTIONS, STEMS, OR FRAMES | OUTLINE AND RATIONALE |
|---|---|---|
| Ask teacher to reflect on his or her area of focus. | • What are you learning about your area of focus?<br>• What have you tried?<br>• How has student learning improved as a result of what you have tried?<br>• Tell me what is happening in the next two to three weeks in terms of your area of focus. | Clarifying and reviewing the teacher's learning on the teacher's area of focus helps to get clarity on how this focus will be studied during the targeted feedback cycle. |
| Decide together on observable evidence and set teacher and student outcomes. | • What will the student result be at the end of this observation and feedback cycle?<br>• What evidence should we observe for (in relation to change in your practice and student learning)? | Having agreed-on outcomes ahead of time narrows the observation and strengthens the feedback. |
| Decide together on type and frequency of observation. | • Based on the outcomes, it seems like I should come in …<br>• What kind of feedback would you like during the next two to three weeks? | Doing this ahead of time prepares the teacher and the principal for the amount of time required to meet the goals of the targeted feedback cycle. |
| Commit to follow up and plan first visit. | Alright, so I'll see you … | Being specific about follow-up creates a credible system for observation and feedback that the teacher and principal can rely on. |

*Source:* © 2014 University of Washington Center for Educational Leadership.

# Table 6.2
## Affirmation conversation

Conversations with a teacher are situated within a cycle of teacher learning. Therefore, there are multiple types of conversations. The purpose of an affirmation conversation is to quickly validate and support implementation of new practice.

- The *primary* purpose of ongoing classroom observations is not to judge the quality of teachers but to find the most effective way to support teachers' growth.
- Frequent observation leads to *less,* not more, apprehension (Marzano, Frontier, & Livingston, 2011).

| STEPS | POSSIBLE QUESTIONS, STEMS, AND FRAMES | OUTLINE AND RATIONALE |
|---|---|---|
| Set the context, if needed. | • As you know, the way I'm observing and giving feedback is changing.<br>• The purpose of this conversation is to …<br>• By the end of the conversation, I hope we will … | Setting the context for targeted observation and feedback helps to make the purpose of the affirmation conversation transparent. |
| Share evidence. | • I noticed the following three things in relation to your area of focus …<br>• The work you did on ___ resulted in the following student learning … | Sharing two to three pieces of evidence from observation of the teacher's area of focus confirms the teacher's current level of practice. |
| Offer quick confirmations or feedback. | • Keep going!<br>• Keep going and let's have a longer conversation next time to see what's next. | By quickly confirming a new practice, you are validating the teacher's work and emphasizing continuous improvement. |

*Source:* © 2014 University of Washington Center for Educational Leadership.

## Table 6.3
## Next step conversation

Conversations with a teacher are situated within a cycle of teacher learning. Therefore, there are multiple types of conversations. The purpose of the next step conversation is to follow up on implementation and to think through a next step with the teacher.

- The *primary* purpose of ongoing classroom observations is not to judge the quality of teachers but to find the most effective way to support teachers' growth.
- Frequent observation leads to *less*, not more, apprehension (Marzano, Frontier, & Livingston, 2011).

| STEPS | POSSIBLE QUESTIONS, STEMS, AND FRAMES | OUTLINE AND RATIONALE |
|---|---|---|
| Set the context, if needed. | • As you know, the way I'm observing and giving feedback is changing.<br>• The purpose of this conversation is to …<br>• By the end of the conversation, I hope we will … | Setting the context for targeted observation and feedback helps to make the purpose of the next step conversation transparent. |
| Share evidence. | • I noticed the following three things in relation to your area of focus …<br>• The work you did on ___ resulted in the following student learning … | Sharing two to three pieces of evidence from observation of the teacher's area of focus confirms the teacher's current level of practice. |
| Ask for teacher responses in relation to his or her area of focus and ask for teacher's next step. | • What are you learning about the teaching practice you are engaged in?<br>• What are you noticing about your students?<br>• What's next? | By tying the change in teacher practice to student learning, the principal is confirming the relationship between change in practice and student learning. This is also an opportunity for the teacher to share what he or she will do next. |

*(continued)*

**Table 6.3**

*(continued)*

| STEPS | POSSIBLE QUESTIONS, STEMS, AND FRAMES | OUTLINE AND RATIONALE |
|-------|----------------------------------------|------------------------|
| *If teacher is unsure of next step:* | | |
| Provide a next step if teacher doesn't decide on a next step. | Try this _____tomorrow. | By providing specific suggestions or a next step, you are confirming the teacher's work and emphasizing continuous improvement. If a teacher is struggling to come up with a next step, go ahead and share your ideas. |
| *Make sure you end the conversation with this:* | | |
| Commit to follow up. | Great. I'll see you __ to see how the next step in your practice is going. Thanks! | Close the conversation by setting up the next observation or follow-up plan. |

*Source:* © 2014 University of Washington Center for Educational Leadership.

## Table 6.4
## Reflection conversation

Conversations with a teacher are situated within a cycle of teacher learning. Therefore, there are multiple types of conversations. The purpose of a reflection conversation is to share evidence of teacher and student learning and to decide on next steps for independent and collaborative study.

- The *primary* purpose of ongoing classroom observations is not to judge the quality of teachers but to find the most effective way to support teachers' growth.
- Frequent observation leads to *less,* not more, apprehension (Marzano, Frontier, & Livingston, 2011).

| STEPS | POSSIBLE QUESTIONS, STEMS, OR FRAMES | OUTLINE AND RATIONALE |
|---|---|---|
| Set the context, if needed. | • As you know, the way I'm observing and giving feedback is changing.<br>• The purpose of this conversation is to ...<br>• By the end of the conversation, I hope we will ... | Setting the context for targeted observation and feedback makes the purpose of the reflection conversation transparent. |
| Review the district and school goals and teacher's area of focus (based on the instructional framework). | • As a school, we're working on ...<br>• Your area of focus is ...<br>• Here's how it sits within the instructional framework ... | Creating coherence on the school goals, district goals, and the instructional framework situates the teacher's area of focus within a larger context. |
| Ask the teacher about what he or she has learned about his or her area of focus. Ask what the teacher has noticed about student learning. | • What did you learn about your area of focus within this cycle?<br>• What changes have you made in your practice?<br>• What is the impact of what you have tried on student learning? | Asking the teacher about his or her overall learning within the targeted feedback cycle helps the teacher synthesize his or her learning and bring forward the changes in practice that have resulted in student learning. |

*(continued)*

## Table 6.4

*(continued)*

| STEPS | POSSIBLE QUESTIONS, STEMS, OR FRAMES | OUTLINE AND RATIONALE |
|---|---|---|
| Share evidence from observations of area of focus that had the biggest impact on student learning. | • The work you did on ___ resulted in the students learning ____. | Synthesizing and sharing evidence that highlights the changes a teacher has made that has resulted in student learning helps the teacher decide on what to continue to work on and study. |
| Ask about the teacher's next steps for independent and collaborative study. | • What's next?<br>• How are you going to continue studying your area of focus?<br>• What are you going to look for as evidence of student learning? | Asking the teacher about next steps helps the principal consider how he or she will organize professional development. It also helps the teacher decide how to study and learn with colleagues. |
| Commit to the next targeted feedback cycle. | Keep me in the loop about what you continue to learn about your area of focus, and we'll have another targeted feedback cycle in a few months. | Suggesting when the teacher might be a part of another cycle helps the teacher consider the support he or she will need from colleagues and how to continue to study. The principal will be accountable for following up and connecting the targeted feedback cycles. |

*Source:* © 2014 University of Washington Center for Educational Leadership.

# A Call for System Action to Support Principals as Instructional Leaders

Mountain View Middle School does not exist in isolation. Although Rachel is the leader of the school, she is also one of more than 50 principals in her urban school district. As Rachel shapes her leadership role to support teacher professional learning, she too is actively learning through her own participation in a middle school principal network, along with one-on-one coaching from her principal supervisor. There is a distinct role that school districts can and must play in the design and implementation of a learning system that supports the improvement of practice from the classroom to the district office. This chapter focuses on the role of the district in supporting Rachel's leadership efforts described in the preceding chapters.

## RECIPROCAL ACCOUNTABILITY

The foundational idea of reciprocal accountability is evident in Rachel's leadership work with the teachers at Mountain View Middle School. Rachel understands that her job as a leader is to ensure that teachers have the knowledge, skills, and expertise necessary to improve their instructional practice. This idea of reciprocity is not exclusive to the school site. In fact, we think the design of a true learning system must be grounded in a reciprocal through line that runs from the classroom to the school district office. Evidence of this through line should be apparent at all levels of the system. Just as teachers know each of their students as learners so that they can support their learning in differentiated ways, principals need to know their teachers, and district leaders need to know their principals. This through line is explicitly designed to support learning at all levels of the system, and the measurement of that learning is the actual improvement of practice and ultimately student learning.

When we speak about the idea of reciprocal accountability in our work across the country, school and district leaders heartedly nod their heads in agreement. At a fundamental level, folks know that it is irresponsible to hold someone accountable for something that they don't know how to do. The larger challenge is how to design and resource a system that truly supports learning at all levels and that provides the conditions and supports to enable that learning to be actualized in daily practice. And with respect to the job of the school principal, that learning system must address three challenges we see in school districts—small and large—across the country.

## THREE CHALLENGES

Rachel is only one of more than 100,000 school principals in the United States who sit at a critical intersection of increased accountability. Although it is widely understood that principals play a pivotal role in the improvement of teaching and learning, districts have to pay attention to creating the necessary conditions for principal success. We have observed that principals experience three primary challenges that impact their effectiveness as instructional leaders. First, many principals work in systems that have not developed a common understanding of the day-to-day work that principals should be engaged in to improve teaching practice and student learning at scale. Second, principals may not receive the intensive, coordinated, and embedded professional learning they need to improve their skills. Third, districts may not provide principals with the time and support they need on a daily basis to engage with teachers and students focusing on the improvement of teaching and learning.

## ADDRESSING THE CHALLENGES: THE PRINCIPAL SUPPORT FRAMEWORK

Thousands of school leaders across the country face these challenges in their schools every day. Although Rachel, too, has her share of challenges due to the everyday demands of the job, she is fortunate to work in a district that thoughtfully determines what principals need in order to be effective and then deliberately designs strategies to meet those needs. The district's work is guided by the Principal Support Framework (PSF), developed at the Center for Educational Leadership as part of a larger, Leading for Effective Teaching project funded by the Bill & Melinda Gates Foundation. (To learn more about the Leading for Effective Teaching project, go to https://www.k-12leadership.org/bill-melinda-gates-foundation-leading-effective-teaching. The complete PSF can be found in Table 7.1 at the end of this chapter). In what follows, we will describe the three action areas found in the PSF and highlight examples from our case study to help illustrate its concepts.

## PSF Action Area 1: A Shared Vision of Principals as Instructional Leaders

### Goal

Principals understand the school system's expectations for their roles and effective practices as school instructional leaders. These expectations guide the work principals perform day to day, and the practices can be sustained over time.

### Vision

- High-priority practices of instructional leaders drive the day-to-day work of principals.
- High-priority practices of instructional leaders drive the professional development of principals.
- School system leaders understand and communicate broadly and uniformly the vision of instructional leadership.
- Principals are hired based on criteria and processes aligned to the research-based practices of instructional leadership.
- Principals assess and measure their own performance in relation to high-priority instructional leadership practices defined by their district.
- Personnel decisions are determined by principal performance measures in alignment with high-priority instructional leadership practices.

This action area calls for a school system to define, clearly and in detail, what it expects principals to do as the instructional leaders of their schools. Although most states have adopted new principal evaluation systems and performance rubrics, these may not provide principals clear direction on the highest-priority activities they should be involved in on a day-to-day basis. In the case of Rachel's school district, this means engaging with principals in a process to develop a consensus on the principal practices that will be most emphasized in their professional development and evaluation. Principals review the state principal evaluation rubric along with broader research, discuss what is working in their schools, and engage in a districtwide conversation on what matters most in their work. As a result, central office leaders and principals agree on a set of high-priority leadership standards as the focus of their work together. These standards are intended to emphasize those leadership practices most closely linked to the improvement of teaching and learning.

## PSF Action Area 2: A System of Support for Developing Principals as Instructional Leaders

### Goal

Principals have the skills, tools, and support that they need to grow and successfully apply the system's high-priority instructional leadership practices.

### Vision

- Principals receive the tools, targeted professional development, and other support they need to apply the high-priority instructional leadership practices in their day-to-day work as instructional leaders.

- Principals work with principal supervisors to be able to provide differentiated support through teaching, modeling, and coaching.

- Principals have ownership for driving and prioritizing their own growth and improvement as instructional leaders.

- The work of principal supervisors, staff providing professional development, and others supporting principal growth is coordinated and tightly aligned to developing principals as instructional leaders.

- Principals are engaged in collaboration with other principal colleagues to improve practice and rely on each other as support and resources.

At the heart of action area 2 is creating a learning system that supports principals' growth as instructional leaders. The key ideas that underlie this action area include fostering differentiated support for principals as instructional leaders, fostering principals' agency and ownership of their learning process, and ensuring the authenticity of the work and learning between principals and the district support.

With guidance and grounding from the Council of Chief State School Officers (CCSSO) Model Principal Supervisor Standards (2015), districts across the country are revising or creating new roles for central office leaders who can provide focused support for principals' growth as instructional leaders. Prior to the opening of Mountain View Middle School, Rachel's school district had also revised the principal supervisor position so that the person in that role would be responsible for the evaluation of principals and for helping them improve their leadership practice through direct teaching and coaching. In what follows, we illustrate how Rachel's supervisor, Daphne dedicates time to coach and support Rachel as an instructional leader, how Daphne gathers evidence to guide her coaching decisions, and how she advocates for policies and strategies to support Mountain View's success.

Given the district's newly revised role, Daphne is expected to be in schools working side by side with principals 70% of her time, focusing mainly on the agreed-on high-priority standards discussed in action area 1. Daphne uses several evidence-gathering methods to help her consider Rachel's knowledge, skills, and expertise. These methods include direct observation of staff meetings and professional development work, engaging in data-focused discussions with Rachel about student performance, participating in learning walkthroughs in classrooms, and using several specific tools including frameworks, protocols, instructional guides, and rubrics. Such evidence-gathering methods enable Daphne to develop an understanding of Rachel's current capabilities and her learning needs. (For a deeper look into CEL's Gathering Evidence for 4 Dimensions of Principal Instructional Leadership, refer to Appendix 1 at the end of the book.)

**Teaching and Coaching**  The idea of teaching and coaching transcends the traditional view of the principal supervisor role from purely monitoring and evaluating to working alongside the principal to provide differentiated support for specific problems of leadership practice in a way that ensures co-ownership of the improvement efforts. The key to the success of this work is ensuring that the problem(s) of practice are real and of urgency to the principal and that the principal supervisor and principal agree on the focus for their work together. As we saw in Chapter 2, Rachel's problem of practice evolved over time, changing distinctly between the planning year and the subsequent years of the school's existence. This required the work between Rachel and Daphne to change and evolve as well. In the earliest part of their coaching relationship, their work together focused solely on the vision and culture of the school, emphasizing how to engage staff members and the school community in developing a vision with a clear direction for academic success for *every* student. The *every* student was particularly operative in this case, given that the new school merged a program for the district-wide gifted and talented students with neighborhood students.

As the vision and culture of the school becomes more firmly established, Daphne and Rachel's work shifts to other aspects of Rachel's instructional leadership practice, including supporting teacher growth using ongoing feedback. With the idea that every teacher can continue to improve practice, Rachel understands the power of teacher feedback cycles and wants to improve her skills at providing useful, growth-oriented feedback to teachers so that she can then support her assistant principals in honing their feedback skills. For example, Rachel and several other middle school principals with a similar learning goal have formed a small learning cohort. Every four to six weeks, the cohort members submit a video of a feedback conversation with a teacher. As we discuss in Chapter 6, it is important to note that for feedback to be useful to teachers, it needs to reflect a problem of teaching practice that the teacher is interested in focusing on and for which the teacher is already on the verge of fully incorporating into his or her practice. With all of the good work that Rachel had already done building a staff learning culture that is public and collaborative, it is easy to find teachers willing to support Rachel's own learning.

During the review of Rachel's feedback conversation, Daphne pushes in as appropriate and models specific conversational architectures that teachers would find most insightful and supportive. Daphne relies on others in the cohort to also model when appropriate. In this way Daphne has been able to seize on the varying levels of feedback expertise among the other principals. Over the next several months, Rachel has continued to provide targeted feedback to teachers and videoed a number of those feedback sessions. Then during their regular check-in, Daphne reviews and debriefs the feedback sessions. As Rachel deepens her feedback expertise, she then works with her assistant principals to develop and support their learning using a similar learning format. The extension of that learning is evident in Chapter 6 in Nadia's feedback cycles with the math teachers.

Daphne's work with Rachel has been guided by the use of an inquiry cycle tool—a structured process to codevelop a focus on specific problems of leadership practice, the design of a learning plan for the principal, and a way to analyze the impact of the learning. The essence of the inquiry cycle tool is the co-owned and authentic problem of practice that the principal supervisor and principal work on together. (For a deeper look into CEL's Inquiry Cycle Tool, refer to Appendix 2 at the end of the book.)

**Communication from and to the Central Office**  By nature of her place and role in the district's organizational hierarchy, Daphne serves as an important conduit for two-way communication between the central office and individual principals. This can be tricky for principal supervisors. They often feel stuck in the middle between school board and district policy initiatives and the day-to-day realities that principals face in the leadership of their schools. Daphne navigates this tension by simultaneously (1) helping principals more fully understand how the improvement work in their own schools is linked to and supported by the broader school district strategic goals and (2) buffering and brokering for the principal as necessary (for more on the ideas of buffering and brokering, please see Honig, 2012).

For Mountain View Middle School, Daphne brokers additional monetary resources to support the planning and implementation year of the reopened school and she works with the district office to earmark enough budgetary monies to hire Rachel an entire year before she opens the school. Daphne works with the teachers' union to address the hiring process for Mountain View Middle School. Their teachers' union contract, similar to most contracts, has specific teacher transfer rules in place pertaining to existing schools. The transfer rules largely invoke teacher seniority as the determining factor in school transfer cases. Mountain View Middle School's circumstances, as a new school for an expanding student population and a school serving an existing group of students from various feeder elementary schools, poses questions about how the transfer rules would apply. Daphne has worked extensively with other district officials and the teachers' union to develop a memorandum of understanding (MOU) that governed how Mountain View Middle School would be staffed. The MOU struck a balance between new hiring and transfers that enables Rachel to preemptively hire a group of five teachers and one counselor during the planning year that would form a core group moving forward.

Daphne has performed an important buffering role when necessary. At the time that Mountain View Middle School was set to open, the district had previously invested heavily in the creation of PLCs for each school to the point that there was, in policy, an expectation that every school had an operating PLC that met specific structural and process guidelines. However, given that Rachel was opening a new school, she didn't think that PLCs were the right first step. As we saw in Chapter 2, Rachel first needed to establish a whole school vision, identify what they valued in professional learning, what they were looking for instructionally in the classrooms, and what their common formative assessments were going to be. As Rachel expressed to Daphne, there were lots of parts that were needed before teachers could even get to that specific model of PLCs. Fortunately, Daphne agreed with the argument and could buffer the district expectation so that Rachel had the time and space to do the important visioning work before investing staff time in PLCs.

### PSF Action Area 3: A Strategic Partnership Between the Central Office and Principals

**Goal**

The central office delivers effective, integrated support and services that increase the ability of principals to successfully lead their schools.

**Vision**

- Schools receive differentiated and integrated services rooted in an understanding of the needs of each school.
- Central office services are designed to anticipate and proactively meet the needs of each school.
- Central office relationships with principals add value to the work of the principal and school.
- The central office has a culture of continuous improvement and can learn, adapt, and respond to the changing needs of schools.
- There is an efficiency created by a well-coordinated and defined set of operational systems.

Imagine a school system that provides principals full clarity about their daily practice along with robust professional development to improve their performance but does nothing to change the actual overall administrative responsibilities and commitments required of principals and those who directly supervise and support those principals. Action area 3 addresses this situation by focusing central office action on the overwhelming demands placed on principals. Districts engaged in this action area take seriously the issue that principals do not have enough time in their day to be effective instructional leaders. These districts require principals to attend fewer district meetings, provide more efficient and strategic support from the central office, and invest in teacher leaders who can share instructional leadership responsibilities.

Previously, we saw how Daphne engaged in very specific strategies designed to support Rachel's learning and improvement. This did not happen by accident. Rachel's district invested heavily in revising the principal supervisor role (a sample job description for this type of role can be found in Figure 7.1 at the end of this chapter). Historically, the role of the principal supervisor in Rachel's district was an amalgam: they were responsible for supervising 20 schools and had large spans of responsibility that included, among other things, serving on district collective bargaining committees, various program responsibilities, district boundary committees, and a range of community responsibilities and engagements. The role was designed, perhaps unintentionally, to be a problem-solver and crises interventionist but not to lead and support the development of principals as instructional leaders.

**District Area Leadership Teams**   Rachel's district created cross-department, district area leadership teams to ensure principals receive integrated and coordinated support from central office departments. Historically, each central office department, for example, special education, transportation, facilities, curriculum, and so on, communicated expectations directly to the school sites in a wholly uncoordinated way. This has resulted in principals being bombarded with dozens of daily emails or phone calls from central office units asking for or requiring an immediate response. Principals are often chasing their proverbial tails doing all kinds of tasks that had nothing to do with improving the quality of teaching and learning in their schools. Under the new arrangement, central office unit heads meet once a month with Daphne and the other principal supervisors to discuss how best to support schools, knowing they have to strike a balance between external policy demands (federal, state, and district) and learning about what schools need in order to feel well supported. Under this arrangement, individual program unit heads are not allowed to individually require principals to attend a meeting, nor are they allowed to individually communicate unit demands to principals. All written communications need to be sent to the schools as part of a weekly coordinated information packet. Any necessary face-to-face time is relegated to a short (90-minute) management meeting once a month. All other meetings between the principal supervisors and principals are expected to focus on the kind of supported professional learning previously outlined.

**More Personalized Hiring Practices**   A school district's human resources office ensures that established procedures and routines are in place and followed across the entire system. With respect to hiring practices, this can manifest as the HR office playing a gatekeeper role versus a more personalized service role. For example, previously in Rachel's district, all school principals followed the same staff hiring process. Once there was an opening, the principal contacted the HR office to post a position. HR ensured the budget authorization to fill the position, applied appropriate collective bargaining agreements in terms of transfer requests, and eventually posted a position. Given the large size of Rachel's district, multiple positions were typically posted that served multiple schools at once. This process was efficient, compliant with all necessary rules and agreements, and treated each school equally.

Under the district's new focus of creating a reciprocal through line, the HR department is tasked with coming up with a more individual school approach to hiring while adhering to all of the necessary rules and regulations. This results in an HR official joining the monthly meeting with Daphne and the other principal supervisors to gain a deeper understanding of the schools in each area and how best to serve each school's hiring (and other HR) needs. Now, rather than simply posting a position and given a generic file of applicants, principals are asked first to speak with an HR official about the particular needs of that position. For example, when Rachel needed to hire a new math teacher in year four to join an already well-established math team that had completely opened up their classroom practice, she was able to communicate the more nuanced needs of that position to the HR official. And because the HR official had been routinely attending the monthly meeting with Daphne, she already knew of Rachel's heavy focus on embedded professional learning. In this way, the HR official was able to highlight specific candidates that might fit well at Rachel's school, versus just handing her a folder of all middle school math applicants.

**Central Office Learning**   The idea of continuous improvement is a key underpinning of action area 3. As such, learning is continuously emphasized and supported in Rachel's school district central office, including focused support for the principal supervisors. Learning how to shift from a purely supervisory stance to a coaching and teaching stance means that principal supervisors are also working on their practice. Daphne and the other principal supervisors, as well as other division and department heads, each have his or her own individual learning plan for the year. Just as for the principals, the learning plan has been developed based on real, authentic problems of leadership practice and is wholly supported by the leader's direct supervisor. Professional learning networks within the central office have been formed to support individual and group learning. In this way, Rachel's school district has established a learning through line that goes from the classroom to the district office.

The Principal Support Framework provides a starting point and guide for clarifying the role of principal as instructional leader, for considering how principals can receive differentiated support for their learning—based on their authentic needs—from someone who can learn and teach alongside them, and for considering how to reduce the demands placed on principals that take them away from instructional leadership. Without systems action, the kind of deep professional learning exemplified in the previous chapters might happen by chance with a heroic principal at the helm of the school, but it could not be maintained or scaled to other schools across the district. The Principal Support Framework provides a blueprint for the kind of systems action necessary to support learning at all levels of the school system.

## DISCUSSION QUESTIONS

1. To what extent is there a consensus in your school district regarding the high-priority leadership practices principals should be engaged in everyday to increase student learning?

2. How does your school district differentiate the learning and support of school principals?

3. What systems, structures, and strategies does your school system have in place to support principal instructional leadership?

## REFERENCES

Council of Chief State School Officers (CCSSO). (2015). *Model principal supervisor standards.* Washington, DC: Author.

Honig, M. (2012). District central office leadership as teaching: How central office administrators support principals' development as instructional leaders. *Educational Administration Quarterly, 48*(4).

## Table 7.1
## Principal Support Framework (Version 2.0)

The Principal Support Framework describes key actions of central offices that effectively support principals as instructional leaders. Based upon a broad understanding of how principals work to improve teaching and learning at scale, this framework provides guidance so that central office leaders can do the following:

- Develop a vision of what it means to support principals.
- Assess and determine strengths and next steps in their school system's approach to supporting principals as instructional leaders.
- Surface technical assistance needs.
- Highlight areas for inquiry and next-stage policy development.

| ACTION AREA | THE VISION | GUIDING QUESTIONS |
|---|---|---|
| **Action Area 1: A Shared Vision of Principals as Instructional Leaders**<br><br>The school system has defined, clearly and in detail, what it expects principals to do as the instructional leaders of their schools. It selects and evaluates principals based primarily on whether they can successfully execute those practices.<br><br>**Goal:** Principals understand the school system's expectations for their roles and effective practices as school instructional leaders. These expectations guide the work principals perform day to day, and the practices can be sustained over time. | • High-priority practices of instructional leaders drive the day-to-day work of principals.<br>• High-priority practices of instructional leaders drive the professional development of principals.<br>• School system leaders understand and communicate both broadly and uniformly the vision of instructional leadership.<br>• Principals are hired based on criteria and processes aligned to the research-based practices of instructional leadership.<br>• Principals assess and measure their own performance in relation to high-priority instructional leadership practices defined by their district. | 1. In what ways do high-priority instructional leadership practices drive principal goal setting and professional development?<br>2. To what extent is principal evaluation driven by researched-based practices?<br>3. How do high-priority instructional leadership practices guide candidate acceptance into the principal hiring pipeline and the selection and placement of principals?<br>4. How do principals and supervisors access data on principal performance in relation to high-priority instructional leadership practices? |

**Table 7.1**
*(continued)*

| ACTION AREA | THE VISION | GUIDING QUESTIONS |
|---|---|---|
| | • Personnel decisions are determined by principal performance measures in alignment with high-priority instructional leadership practices. | 5. How does principal performance in relation to high-priority instructional leadership practices impact retention and career ladder opportunities for principals?<br><br>6. To what extent do principals' calendars reflect an emphasis on high-priority instructional leadership practices?<br><br>7. In what ways do school system leaders communicate the role of principals as instructional leaders? |
| **Action Area 2: A System of Support for Developing Principals as Instructional Leaders**<br><br>The school system has created a system of differentiated and targeted support to develop principals' growth as instructional leaders.<br><br>**Goal:** Principals have the skills, tools and support that they need to grow and successfully apply the system's high-priority instructional leadership practices. | • Principals receive the tools, targeted professional development and other support they need to apply the high-priority instructional leadership practices into their day-to-day work as instructional leaders.<br><br>• Principals work with principal supervisors able to provide differentiated support through teaching, modeling and coaching. | 1. To what extent do principals receive differentiated support focused on their development as instructional leaders?<br><br>2. How does the school system ensure that principal supervisors have the requisite skills and disposition to support principals' growth as instructional leaders? |

*(continued)*

**Table 7.1**
*(continued)*

| ACTION AREA | THE VISION | GUIDING QUESTIONS |
|---|---|---|
| | • Principals have owner-ship for driving and prioritizing their own growth and improve-ment as instruc-tional leaders.<br><br>• The work of princi-pal supervisors, staff providing professional development, and oth-ers supporting principal growth is coordinated and tightly aligned to developing principals as instructional leaders.<br><br>• Principals are engaged in collaboration with other principal col-leagues to improve practice and rely on each other as support and resources. | 3. To what extent do principals have frequent opportunities to access and utilize each other as resources for learning and performance improvement?<br><br>4. In what ways do principals have access to quality professional development tools and resources needed to improve their performance?<br><br>5. How do principal supervisors collaborate with other central office staff to align systems and resources to support principals as instructional leaders?<br><br>6. To what extent is principal supervisor evaluation tied directly to the instructional leadership success of the principals being supported?<br><br>7. To what extent are principal supervisors able to prioritize working with principals as the day-to-day focus of their work? |

**Table 7.1**
*(continued)*

| ACTION AREA | THE VISION | GUIDING QUESTIONS |
|---|---|---|
| | | 8. To what extent do principal supervisors receive the resources, support and professional development they need to successfully support principals as instructional leaders? |
| **Action Area 3: A Strategic Partnership Between the Central Office and Principals**<br><br>The central office develops systemic solutions that ensure instructional leadership is the primary job of principals.<br><br>**Goal:** The central office delivers effective, integrated support and services that increase the ability of principals to successfully lead their schools. | • Schools receive differentiated and integrated services rooted in an understanding of the needs of each school.<br><br>• Central office services are designed to anticipate and proactively meet the needs of each school.<br><br>• Central office relationships with principals add value to the work of the principal and school.<br><br>• The central office has a culture of continuous improvement and can learn, adapt and respond to the changing needs of schools.<br><br>• There is an efficiency created by a well-coordinated and defined set of operational systems. | 1. To what extent can central office staff articulate the connection between their work and supporting principals as instructional leaders?<br><br>2. How does the central office provide differentiated and integrated service to schools rooted in an understanding of the needs of each school?<br><br>3. How do high-priority instructional leadership practices and an underlying theory of action guide decisions about principal responsibility and what responsibilities are streamlined or deprioritized?<br><br>4. To what extent are central office teams equipped with the skills and tools to do their jobs? |

*(continued)*

## Table 7.1
*(continued)*

| ACTION AREA | THE VISION | GUIDING QUESTIONS |
|---|---|---|
| | | 5. How does the school system invest in developing the skills of central office staff? |
| | | 6. To what extent are central office staff members empowered to innovate services to better support principals as instructional leaders? |
| | | 7. How does the central office assess its performance at making it possible for principals to spend the majority of their time focused on instructional leadership? |

*Source*: © 2016 University of Washington Center for Educational Leadership. To order copies or request permission to reproduce materials, email edlead@uw.edu, call the Center for Educational Leadership at 206-221-6881 or go to www.K-12leadership.org. No part of this publication may be reproduced, stored in a retrieval system, used in a spreadsheet or transmitted in any form or by any means—electronic, mechanical, photocopying, recording or otherwise—without permission of the Center for Educational Leadership.

---

**Figure 7.1**
**Sample job description for instructional leadership director**

---

**JOB DESCRIPTION**
**Instructional Leadership Director**

**Position Summary**

The West Plainfield School District (WPSD) is committed to helping all of its students learn at high levels. Although many factors affect student learning, the district's ability to support high-quality teaching in every classroom is essential to realizing that goal. Research indicates that principals play a primary role in the improvement of teaching at scale. To that end, WPSD is intensively focusing its central office on improving how it recruits, selects, and develops the highest-quality principals. A hallmark of this initiative involves assigning each principal a senior-level central office leader who is responsible for his or her development as an instructional leader. This marks the district's transition from a heavy emphasis on supervising and monitoring principal performance to one of teaching and coaching as the primary mode of improving performance.

WPSD seeks experienced and successful instructional leaders to serve as **instructional leadership directors** (ILDs). This senior executive-level central office position is designed to be a master teacher of principals, helping them increase their instructional leadership capacities as a means of improving teaching and learning in each school. ILDs' main charge is to use best practices in developing instructional leaders by working with principals one-on-one and in groups. ILDs will spend 100% of their time on this responsibility. Performance in this position will be measured through growth in principal performance and student learning.

**Key Responsibilities**

1. Work one-on-one with principals as partners to grow their instructional leadership capacity.

2. Develop principal professional learning networks focused on principals' growth as instructional leaders.

3. Provide and broker professional development for principals based on individual and group learning needs.

*(continued)*

A Call for System Action to Support Principals as Instructional Leaders    **121**

**Figure 7.1**

(*continued*)

4. Collaborate with ILD colleagues to share ideas and provide coherent support to principals.

5. Collaborate with other units in the central office to provide necessary resources to support principals' instructional leadership.

**Desired Qualifications**

1. Proven ability as a master teacher of adults, especially in K–12 environments, including modeling effective teaching and leadership practices, articulating a vision for effective instruction, creating learning networks, and inviting critique of own practice and reflecting on it.

2. Expert in using evidence of principal and school performance to drive feedback to and teaching of principals, including observing and analyzing principal practice; using data on student, teacher, and principal performance to determine underlying causes; and providing differentiated support based on evidence.

3. Highly skilled at organizing and prioritizing in a demanding context to maximize teaching time with principals, including time management skills and an ability to schedule based on short- and long-term principal learning needs.

4. Proven ability in collaborating and negotiating with central office colleagues in support of principals' instructional leadership efforts, including an understanding of the key roles and responsibilities in the central office, knowledge of how resources are allocated to schools, and an ability to communicate principals' needs to a variety of stakeholders.

**Preferred Background and Work Experiences**

- Successful principalship including recruiting, hiring, supporting, and holding staff members accountable for results
- Demonstrated experience closing gaps in student achievement
- Successful experiences collecting, organizing, and using student and teacher data

**Figure 7.1**

*(continued)*

- Successful experience working with and teaching adults
- Successful experience coaching principals
- Successful district central office experience

# Conclusion

As standards and aspirations rise for what students should know and do, we must create the conditions for adult learning that will enable teachers to make significant shifts in their practice. Developing expertise and skills that deepen over time requires a culture of continuous improvement—supported by the conditions for deliberate practice in which norms of risk-taking, feedback, and coaching prevail. The creation and maintenance of such a culture demands leaders' attention to their reciprocal role in teachers' learning—how to get better together. In this book, we illustrate how the principal of Mountain View Middle School learns with and from the math department teachers, including the explicit leadership role she plays. In particular, we demonstrate how her use of practical processes and tools helps create a culture of problem-solving in order to continuously improve on behalf of students.

Let's take a look at the final math studio for the year, when Andrea, the leadership team, and the math department teachers are preparing for a lesson in Samantha's class. As you read this vignette of their planning session, note the expertise that has been developed within the group and the way the group engages in collective problem-solving. A culture of continuous improvement has taken shape at Mountain View Middle School, where leaders and teachers work together to solve problems of student learning. Leadership has spread across the department as shown by the assistant principal and the department chairs taking an increasingly visible role in shaping the student learning questions that drive the experience.

It is now early spring and the math department teachers are gathered for their final studio of the year. Spring break is five days away and many students at Mountain View Middle School rush into the hallways with excitement for the upcoming vacation. As the small conference room fills up with the math teachers, they chat about their plans for the upcoming week off, and Rachel can tell they are tired and ready for a chance to catch their breaths. Charts line the walls of the conference room with their department goals and some data from the recent common assessment each grade level has conducted. Copies of *Five Practices for Orchestrating Productive Mathematics Discussions* (Stein & Smith, 2011), a resource for the department, sit on the long table. The window is cracked open so a bit of fresh, cool air fills the space.

Sadie, Diane, Nadia, and Rachel have spent several hours the previous week planning for this professional learning session. The planning includes coaching with individual teachers, conversations with Andrea, and lots of reviewing of student and instructional data. They anticipate a full and productive day with Andrea—with some promising changes in the structure and flow. This will be the first studio session in which Nadia, Sadie, and Diane will lead the majority of the facilitation, drawing on Andrea for content expertise as needed. Perhaps even more significant, this time Samantha (the second-year seventh-grade teacher) will be hosting the studio. After months of coaching and support from Sadie and feedback from Nadia, Samantha has decided she is ready to open her own classroom and practice, including sharing a question that reflects significant growth in her learning.

After the welcome and review of the agenda and specific goals, Nadia sets the tone and purpose for the day: "We look forward to our work today in Samantha's classroom. Samantha is grappling with a significant question of equity in how she groups students and sets them up to all have access to complex mathematical thinking and to participate equally. This is something that we all are trying to figure out, so we look forward to learning with Samantha and her students."

The teachers all nod, and Andrea adds, "You've been working hard as a team to figure out how to create rich tasks that can engage all learners and how to keep them working on those tasks even when the work gets harder."

Sadie adds, "And, it's a big celebration that we are all really trying this. I am seeing in my coaching and in my own classroom that group work with complex tasks takes a long time to plan and set up, but that my students are really getting better at persisting through challenging work—in particular my ELLs. I will turn the conversation over to Samantha so she can share some about the context for today and what she's been learning and figuring out."

Samantha takes a sip of her coffee, looks around the group, and says, "I know I've grown a lot this year. I know some of my students have, too. I see the importance of having rich tasks for groups to work on. It's been a lot of work for me to stop jumping in and saving them when they get stuck, but I think my students are mostly in the place where they keep working in their groups even when it gets hard. They've mostly stopped waiting for me to rescue them and they have learned to rely more on each other and the resources in the classroom. Still, though, I know there are these silent students who kind of sit back and wait for someone in their group to do the hard work. It's not every group or even every day, but I see it and it's frustrating and it shows in their assessments. The students who still don't participate end up struggling when they have to do the work on their own."

Sadie looks at Andrea, who nods. Given the affirmation from Andrea to practice her coaching, Sadie asks Samantha, "What is it you really want from your students in the period we will be seeing today?"

Samantha replies, "I really want them all to participate in their small-group discussion of the task. It's a good task; we worked together as a PLC to design it, and we spent time together anticipating their misconceptions already. I know what to look for when the students start working. I just think some of them still go into the activity expecting to not get it and will just sit there, quietly, not disrupting, but just sitting there."

Sadie asks her, "What have you been trying to help them all engage?"

Samantha replies, sharing her thinking with the team again. "Over the past month I've tried different ways of putting them into groups. I used to do groupings randomly, but I have been so bothered by the students who just sit there and wait for their peers to do the work. I decided that it might make more sense to put them in groups by level. That way I'd have a group that was fine on their own, some in the middle, and then I could support the struggling group. That way the silent strugglers could not check out completely. But I am finding the group with the most struggling students really, really struggled." Sadie nods to encourage Samantha to continue.

"So, I knew that did not work. Their work products, actually, as a class as a whole, were really off the mark when I did leveled groups. Except for that one really high group in each class." She laughs a little, remembering, and others nod again. "After we looked at the data, Sadie helped me put them back in mixed-ability groups. This is the first day of that mixed grouping again. When I was thinking about today's studio, I was thinking about how to make the groups most successful with the task. My idea was to assign a leader in each group who would do the recording for the group while they all worked on the task. I thought I would pick one of the stronger students in each group for that job. Sadie suggested I raise that question today for all of you. We have the task all set, we just need to figure out how to get the group to work together in the best way possible. You see, even though they don't depend on me as much, they still struggle, and sometimes they end up writing a completely wrong answer with no idea that their reasoning does not make sense . . ." She trails off, looks at Sadie, and Sadie looks at Andrea.

Andrea comments, "Samantha, thank you for sharing this problem of practice. I am curious what others are thinking about this."

The teachers immediately start talking to one another about their own struggles with grouping. Nadia cuts in and asks Sadie, "Let's think about this together. What message does that send if you have one of the stronger students—whom they all probably see as strong—literally holding the pen in the group?"

Samantha sighs, "I know. It sends the signal that I already decided who is in charge. But those students are kind of in charge anyway because they are so on top of it."

Nadia asks, "What are the other students likely to do then, today?"

Samantha pauses and looks at her notes and her class roster, which lie in front of her. Andrea asks the group for their input. Bob comments, "I can see more students checking out and letting the leader do the work." Samantha considers this and nods.

After a moment, Samantha replies, "Yes. And I know some of the stronger students will just want to do the work for the group because it's easier."

Nadia adds, "I know this is hard work for us. Your students have made a lot of progress in how they collaborate already this year—many more students are involved than were before. This is the next level of our learning—we really want all students to participate and have access to the math work. And, they need to have the expectation that they are all accountable. I am concerned that if we assign a leader, we may undo some of the good work you have done to create more participation. So, what do we do?"

Andrea suggests that the teachers journal for a few minutes and then share some ideas with a partner. After a few minutes of thinking and talking, the teachers listed out several possible structures, including giving the students a big piece of paper to capture all their thinking, walking around and asking any student in the group to report the group's thinking out, and providing the group with more resources (such as other examples or other versions of the problem) they could access if they got stuck. They thought through pros and cons of each of these ideas.

Andrea offered one more strategy, "I like the idea of the giant poster paper for each group—that sends the message that this problem will require *lots* of thinking and exploring. What if you start the class with a really clear statement about all students being expected to participate in the thinking. We could craft that together. Then, you could give each student in a group a different color pen. We could check for all students participating by making sure that each task includes writing in each color pen. We will tell the students up front this is part of the expectation—that we see everyone's thinking on the chart in a substantive way."

The group collectively decides that Andrea's strategy would be worthwhile to try today. They share their interest in seeing how many students actually participate, and, as Diane points out, "Maybe more students are participating than we think. I know I sometimes make assumptions. This way we will know." There is unanimous agreement about Diane's statement and the group turns its attention to the task itself and their strategy for collecting student data during the lesson.

Samantha seems excited about the upcoming work. She comments, "I like that we are all in this together today! Makes me feel less alone. And, if we all listen and record what we hear students doing, we will really know if this works."

This chapter's vignette does not conclude with "we had lots of learning in those studio classrooms and now we are done!" In fact, after several years of learning together, with an intentional focus and plan to improve the quality of teaching and learning, the leaders and teachers of Mountain View Middle School are poised for further learning.

In this case, they are not satisfied now with some students talking in the small groups, they truly want *all* students to make meaning together—and they want to study the practices that will enable this to happen. The challenge of getting better and developing expertise, at anything, lies in the quality of the ongoing opportunity for deliberate practice, supported by risk-taking, feedback, and coaching. What teachers know how to do will affect their beliefs about what to expect from their students—and teachers' own sense of efficacy about their ability to affect student learning. Leaders are charged with creating conditions that enable teachers to learn together in specific ways. These conditions enable teachers to learn the technical aspects of their craft and deepen their understanding of their content area, and they also enable teachers to take risks together, collectively frame and solve problems of student learning, and develop efficacy as they experiment and try out new techniques.

We start with the assumption that we can all get better, that instructional practice affects student learning, and that our sense of efficacy develops as we gain the expertise that enables us to expect more from our students. At the same time, instructional leaders need to stay vigilant about the riptide effect of the water we swim in, where assumptions and beliefs about students' capacities can go unexamined and whose force we must counter. We need to always consider what it means to get better and to engage in collective problem-solving on behalf of our students, lest the riptide pull us back to our bias and images of "high" and "low" students and their capacity to engage in rigorous tasks. Even after several years of job-embedded professional learning, the math department at Mountain View Middle School still confronts the enduring challenge of high expectations for student learning and how to ensure it.

The fact is, our vision for what students can do will always be a moving target. As we learn more, our aspirations and expectations for students also rise. As we get better and develop more expertise, our ability to affect student learning and our sense of efficacy about our impact also increases. Moving from beliefs about "low" or "high" students means connecting our teaching ability to what students can do. This stance is not easily cultivated nor does it come naturally. Cultivating a culture of continuous learning and improvement means taking the long view: getting better by nourishing and sustaining the conditions for adult learning, keeping our eyes on the prize for each of our students.

## REFERENCE

Stein, M. K., & Smith, M. S. (2011). *Five practices for orchestrating productive mathematics discussions*. Reston, VA: National Council of Teachers of Mathematics.

# Gathering Evidence for 4 Dimensions of Principal Instructional Leadership

Increasingly, school districts across the country are working to create strong learning-focused partnerships between principals and their supervisors. In districts studied for their work on central office transformation, leaders created positions that the researchers called Instructional Leadership Directors (ILDs), executive-level staff charged with spending nearly all their time supporting principals' growth, both one-on-one and in principal training networks. Researchers found that those ILDs (also often known as principal supervisors) whose work was associated with reported and observed progress in principals' instructional leadership approached their work as master teachers of principals: i.e., they engaged in the teaching methods that in other settings are associated with improving practice.

## WHAT THIS TOOL WILL HELP YOU DO.

In our experience, to do such a job well, principal supervisors must become very familiar with their principals' strengths and weaknesses as instructional leaders and attend to their growth over time. We developed this tool to continuously assess principals' instructional leadership; develop a clear sense of what counts as evidence for instructional leadership; and create systems for collecting and organizing evidence of principals' instructional leadership.

---

*Source:* © 2014 University of Washington Center for Educational Leadership.

Adapted from *Principal Instructional Leadership Evidence-Gathering Tool for Instructional Leadership Directors* created by the Center for Educational Leadership and Meredith I. Honig, and commissioned by the Wallace Foundation.

# RESEARCH-BASED TOOLS FOR CENTRAL OFFICE TRANSFORMATION

The tools in this kit were created by the Center for Educational Leadership and Meredith I. Honig, Associate Professor of Education, at the University of Washington. They are based on a groundbreaking study, conducted by Honig and colleagues at the University of Washington, on how three school district central offices undertook to radically transform their central office into a true teaching and learning support system. That study, *Central Office Transformation for District-wide Teaching and Learning Improvement*, funded by the Wallace Foundation, investigated central office transformation efforts in three urban districts. These findings have since been confirmed and elaborated by a follow-up study, conducted by Honig and colleagues, involving six additional districts of varying sizes. In designing the tools we also drew on our direct experience helping districts of various sizes across the country get started with central office transformation.

The tool offers principal supervisors a framework for gauging principals' instructional leadership capacities combined with an instrument for gathering evidence of individual strengths and weaknesses over multiple contacts. Such knowledge is the necessary foundation for continuing work with each principal differentiated for that principal's needs. Critical examination of evidence about principals' leadership, conducted as work, also helps model the use of evidence about teaching and learning for their principals and others throughout the system.

The tool lays out a vision of the principal's role as instructional leader using the Four Dimensions of Instructional Leadership (4D) developed at the Center for Educational Leadership at the University of Washington College of Education. It articulates the core ideas, guiding questions, and possible observables for each dimension, along with specific suggestions for where and how to observe principals' practice, and artifacts that may be helpful to collect in building evidence. The criteria and observables in the tool can and should be evaluated and adapted to meet a district's own criteria for principal leadership.

Broadly, the tool is intended to meet these research-based criteria for success:

1. **Continuously assess instructional leadership.**  Instructional leadership is not reflected in any one-time event; rather, it reflects a stance of working extensively with teachers both inside and outside instructional settings to develop insights and raise questions that lead to further joint actions designed to improve teaching and learning. Principal supervisors need to take a similar stance in the relationships they build with their principals and allow such a disposition to inform and shape continuous instructional leadership improvement.

2. **Develop a clear sense of what counts as evidence for instructional leadership.**  Without a clearly articulated framework to guide their examination of principals' work, it is too easy for practitioners to make claims and develop hunches without specific evidence in mind. Principal supervisors must become smart about both the kind of evidence that would be helpful for their efforts to develop strong mental models of their principals' instructional leadership and ways to assess the quality of such evidence.

3. **Create systems for collecting and organizing evidence of principals' instructional leadership.**  Most would agree that it is hard to have any sort of influence on that which hasn't been noticed and named. Principal supervisors need to have systematic, intentional systems to collect evidence of their principals' instructional leadership in order to develop powerful one-on-one assistance relationships with them in service of better teaching and learning.

We suggest that a facilitator, working with a group of district executive leaders in the principal supervisor role, invite the group, first, to consider and amend the criteria in this tool as needed to align them with any existing district frameworks. Principal supervisors can then begin to use the tool in individual work with principals. Reconvening after a period of time to practice using the tool, it may be useful for principal supervisors to reflect on the following questions:

1. What did you notice about how you have been documenting principals' instructional leadership compared to what the tool prompts you to do? In particular:

2. Were some parts of your observation more elaborated than others? If so, which ones? (That is, do you tend to focus on certain dimensions of principals' instructional leadership more than others?)

3. Do you seem to be privileging certain kinds of evidence over others? For instance, do you mainly collect evidence on teachers' practice or does your evidence elaborate what principals are doing? Do you seem to favor quantitative over qualitative data? Do you seem to get most of your evidence from classroom walkthroughs rather than other sources?

4. As you look over your picture of principals' practice, consider: The tool prompts you to provide evidence in relation to each of the questions. Do your notes include specific pieces of evidence or mostly claims?

5. As you worked with the tool over time, did you find that certain parts of the tool were more useful than others or more important to focus on now with your principals? If so, which ones?

6. How can you make sure that you are doing this evidence gathering *with* principals (rather than to them), as joint work?

7. How do you think you will use the evidence you've been gathering to differentiate your support for these principals?

## 4D INSTRUCTIONAL LEADERSHIP DIMENSION
### VISION, MISSION, AND CULTURE BUILDING

**4D Core Ideas**
(What are the key qualities principal supervisors are trying to get a sense of and further develop in their principals?)

School leaders, committed to collective leadership, create a reflective, equity-driven, achievement-based culture of learning focused upon academic success for every student.

- Through collaboration and shared leadership, staff, students, and the school community embrace a vision of academic success for every student and work toward clear goals focused on student learning.

- School leaders foster a culture of learning, cultural responsiveness, and high expectations for every student and every adult.

- School leaders create and maintain a results-focused learning environment of continuous improvement that is responsive to individual students' needs and the diversity among the students.

**4D Guiding Questions**
(What are the important questions principal supervisors try to ask themselves when developing understanding of those they lead in order to better
teach them?)

1. What do the school's environment and day-to-day interactions among students,
   staff and families say about what is valued in the school community?

2. How does the school leadership communicate and drive the school's instructional agenda?

3. How does the school leadership organize the learning environment to respond
   to cultural and linguistic diversity and the varying learning and social needs
   of students?

4. How do the school leadership and community use evidence of student success and
   learning needs to drive collaboration?

5. How does the school leadership encourage leadership within others?

**Potential Evidence for This Dimension**
(What might a principal supervisor take notice of or pay attention to while
developing an understanding of a principal's current capabilities and learning needs?)

1. Visual representation of the shared vision, mission, goals and progress of the school
   (e.g., hallway displays, school artifacts, documents, academic progress on tests,
   projects attendance, and other school performance measures)

2. Visual representations of the culture of the students and school community

3. Common language among students, staff, and parents when discussing the goals
   and vision of the school and the desired experiences and outcomes for students

4. Staff collaboration and discourse aligned with the school's goals and instructional focus

**Artifacts and documents to consider:**

- School newsletters
- Teacher and student handbooks
- Principal messages to the school and the community
- School's or principal's calendar to see activities planned that reflect celebrations, rituals, traditions, and other events that help to perpetuate culture
- Recordings of student interviews
- Collections of teacher study group documentation
- Digital records of teacher professional learning sessions
- Samples of student work analysis protocols
- Data from student, parent, and staff surveys

---

**Possible Observation Activities**
(How might a principal supervisor go about developing a better sense of where he or she might want to further grow and develop a principal?)

---

1. Notice what is displayed in hallways and classrooms.

2. When talking to anyone in the school community, ask, "What is important here in this school?" "What matters most?"

3. Listen for the level of expectation in student and staff "talk" and whether it reflects high expectations for students and staff.

4. Take note of how the principal uses multiple forms of data (e.g., leading and lagging indicators of student learning and teacher performance) to inform students, staff, and the school community.

5. Take note of how the principal shares the academic performance for the school and the research-based instructional plans being implemented to address the students' needs.

6. Develop awareness of what the staff reads and studies together as evidenced in the principal's professional learning plan.

7. Examine the principal's portfolio or collection of the pertinent information he/she has shared with the staff on improving leading, learning and teaching.

8. Pay attention to the posted or otherwise visible codes of student and adult conduct focused on respect, responsibility, and positive relationships.

# VISION, MISSION, AND CULTURE BUILDING

Observation Notes for Improvement of Learning

**Observation 1**                                        Date: [          ]

[                                                          ]

**Observation 2**                                        Date: [          ]

[                                                          ]

**Observation 3**                                        Date: [          ]

[                                                          ]

**Observation 4**                                        Date: [          ]

[                                                          ]

# 4D INSTRUCTIONAL LEADERSHIP DIMENSION
## IMPROVEMENT OF INSTRUCTIONAL PRACTICE

### 4D Core Ideas
(What are the key qualities principal supervisors are trying to get a sense of and further develop in their principals?)

Based upon a shared vision of effective teaching and learning, school leaders establish a focus on learning; nurture a culture of continuous improvement, innovation and public practice; and develop, monitor, and evaluate teacher performance to improve instruction.

- School leaders use data, evidence and inquiry to analyze student learning as well as to assess both teacher and leadership practice.

- School leaders use a research-based instructional framework to observe teacher practice, engage in cycles of inquiry, and plan individual and collective professional development and coaching needs.

- School leaders use data and evidence of student learning and teacher practice to inform feedback to teachers.

### 4D Guiding Questions
(What are the important questions principal supervisors try to ask themselves when developing understanding of those they lead in order to better teach them?)

1. What evidence is there that school leaders' efforts are resulting in the improvement of teaching practice and student learning?

2. How is leadership distributed to ensure collaboration and collective leadership and that the tasks of instructional leadership are accomplished?

3. What data does the school leadership collect to learn about trends in instructional practice as well as student performance and problems of learning?

4. What is the evidence that among staff there is a shared vision of effective teaching and learning and that the improvement of instructional practice is guided by that vision?

5. What role does a research-based instructional framework play in the observation, analysis, feedback, and inquiry about instructional practice?

6. How does the school leadership use monitoring of instruction and evaluation in the improvement of instruction?

---

**Potential Evidence for This Dimension**
(What might a principal supervisor take notice of or pay attention to while developing an understanding of a principal's current capabilities and learning needs?)

---

1. The principal's portfolio of data that describe:

   a. The strengths and weakness in student performance in relation to Common Core and content standards

   b. The trends in problems of instructional practice across disciplines/grade levels/ populations of students

2. A professional learning plan for staff that is job-embedded and driven by the data on student performance and the school improvement plan

3. The principal's modeling effective practice with staff

4. The principal's use of a variety of data to evaluate teachers

5. The principal's and staff use of data analysis protocols by grade level, department, and whole staff

6. Recent school and classroom data that is posted for staff, students, parents, and other visitors to view

7. Teachers' use of multiple forms of student data to plan instruction

8. Principals conducting frequent observations as reflected in their calendars, journals or other forms of documentation

**Artifacts and documents to consider:**

- Staff use of an instructional framework to ground instructional practice
- Principal's classroom observation and evaluation forms
- School improvement plan
- Professional learning plan
- Agendas from staff meetings/professional learning sessions
- Instructional framework
- Classroom observation form
- School-generated student performance data reports and presentations
- Collection of principal/staff-generated theories of action based on the data analyzed
- Collection of principal/staff-generated reflections about instructional actions they've taken with students and the efficacy of their efforts
- Feedback sheets from staff development sessions or whole faculty study group learning sessions
- Data analysis and student work protocols

---

**Possible Observation Activities**
(How might a principal supervisor go about developing a better sense of where he or she might want to further grow and develop a principal?)

---

1. Talk with students about their learning targets and levels of performance.

2. Observe a professional learning session/staff meeting.

3. Observe video of principal giving feedback to a teacher.

4. Engage in a data-focused discussion with the principal about school and student performance and the instructional plan for improvement in relation to Common Core and content standards.

5. Go on a classroom walkthrough with the principal using the school's instructional framework.

6. Engage in a grade-level or subject-area conversation with principal and teachers planning a unit of study or assessing student understanding.

## IMPROVEMENT OF INSTRUCTIONAL PRACTICE

Observation Notes for Improvement of Learning

**Observation 1**                                      Date: [                    ]

[                                                                              ]

**Observation 2**                                      Date: [                    ]

[                                                                              ]

**Observation 3**                                      Date: [                    ]

[                                                                              ]

**Observation 4**                                      Date: [                    ]

[                                                                              ]

# 4D INSTRUCTIONAL LEADERSHIP DIMENSION
## ALLOCATION OF RESOURCES

### 4D Core Ideas for This Dimension
(What are the key qualities principal supervisors are trying to get a sense of and further develop in their principals?)

School leaders allocate resources strategically so that instructional practice and student learning continue to improve

- School leaders use financial resources, time, facilities, technology, and partnerships innovatively and equitably to accomplish the goal of powerful teaching and learning for all students.
- The school leadership team has articulated clear processes and procedures for instructional support.
- School leaders use data to make equitable decisions about the allocation of resources.

### 4D Guiding Questions
(What are the important questions principal supervisors try to ask themselves when developing understanding of those they lead in order to better teach them?)

1. How does the distribution of resources (i.e., time, money, technology, space, materials, and expertise) relate to improved teaching and learning in this school? What evidence do you have?

2. How do school leaders use instructional coaches, mentors, and other teacher leaders to help improve instructional practice?

3. How are decisions made about staff allocation and student interventions to ensure that the varying needs of students are met?

4. How do school leaders use staff time and collaborative structures to drive the instructional program?

**Potential Evidence for This Dimension**
(What might a principal supervisor take notice of or pay attention to while developing an understanding of a principal's current capabilities and learning needs?)

1. The principal's documentation of the data that drive the equitable allocation of financial, personnel, and instructional support resources:

2. The opportunities for staff collaboration on data analysis, student work, and instructional and intervention planning leading to further instructional actions

3. The principal's annual calendar with key dates for critical school experiences such as interim assessments; topics and dates for professional learning that reflect strategic use of resources

**Artifacts and documents to consider:**

- School budget(s)
- School schedule
- Campus map with programs listed (utilization of space, proximity and location of special classes, etc.)
- Schedule of staff meetings and professional learning sessions
- Allocation of FTE and part-time staffing positions (evidence of equitable distribution of teachers by qualification and experience across levels of coursework)
- Student achievement data disaggregated by student groups, particularly when specific interventions or specialists have been targeted for resources
- Faculty, staff, student, and parent survey data regarding the perceived needs of the school
- Records of professional learning investments (conference attendance, courses remunerated, professional development resourced)
- Memoranda of Understanding or strategic plans with community organizations or other partnerships

**Possible Observation Activities**

(How might a principal supervisor go about developing a better sense of where he or she might want to further grow and develop a principal?)

1. Engage in a discussion with the principal about the school budget and the rationale for his/her allocation of resources.

2. Go on a walkthrough with the principal to observe the use of instructional coaches and other resources-in-action throughout the school.

3. Go on a walkthrough and engage in discussions with principal/teachers on student technology distribution and as learning tool (access in classrooms, depth of use).

4. Talk to teachers about the opportunities for teacher collaboration and planning as well as the resources they need to instruct students well.

5. Observe principal's facilitation with partner groups (PTSA, community organizations, external partners, etc.).

**Allocation of Resources**

Observation Notes for Improvement of Learning

**Observation 1**                                              Date: [                    ]

[                                                                                              ]

**Observation 2**                                              Date: [                    ]

[                                                                                              ]

**Observation 3**                                          Date: [                    ]

[                                                                                    ]

**Observation 4**                                          Date: [                    ]

[                                                                                    ]

# 4D INSTRUCTIONAL LEADERSHIP DIMENSION
## MANAGEMENT OF PEOPLE & PROCESSES

### 4D Core Ideas for This Dimension
(What are the key qualities principal supervisors are trying to get a sense of and further develop in their principals?)

School leaders engage in strategic personnel management and develop working environments in which teachers have full access to supports that help improve instruction.

- School leaders strategically recruit, hire/retain, induct, support, and develop the most qualified staff as well as engage in succession planning.

- School leaders employ critical processes such as planning, implementing, advocating, supporting, communicating, and monitoring to all leadership responsibilities including curriculum, instruction, and school improvement planning.

- School leaders create supportive working environments, which include professional development opportunities, time and space for collaboration, and access to professional learning communities.

---

### 4D Guiding Questions
(What are the important questions principal supervisors try to ask themselves when developing understanding of those they lead in order to better teach them?)

---

1. What evidence exists that the school leadership implements strategic efforts to recruit, hire/retain, induct, support, and develop the best staff?

2. What data and processes does the school leadership use in planning for instructional and school improvement planning?

3. What evidence exists of the staff's access to professional growth opportunities?

---

### Potential Evidence for This Dimension
(What might a principal supervisor take notice of or pay attention to while developing an understanding of a principal's current capabilities and learning needs?)

---

1. The principal's documentation of recruitment strategies, including perceived staffing needs based on student achievement goals

2. The principal's documentation of leadership team meetings that reflect collective and individual thinking for curricular, instructional, and school improvement growth

3. The principal's criteria for professional learning communities (PLCs): how they are formed, how the success of PLCs is measured and celebrated

4. The principal's strategy for differentiated support for teachers using evidence of instructional effectiveness/student learning grounded in an instructional framework

**Artifacts and documents to consider:**

- Building leadership team meeting notes, minutes, and/or other documentation
- Sample interview questions, selection protocols (hiring rubrics), and other associated recruitment/selection documents
- Handouts/PowerPoint slides of professional learning community presentations or teacher learning presentations
- A calendar of professional learning opportunities
- Intake/outtake interview notes for new and/or leaving faculty or staff members

---

**Possible Observation Activities**
(How might a principal supervisor go about developing a better sense of where he or she might want to further grow and develop a principal?)

---

1. Discuss the hiring process employed by the principal, including how he/she influences the applicant pool.

2. Ask a group of teachers how curricular and instructional decisions are made and communicated in this school and by whom.

3. Gather the protocols/resources that principals offer teachers to further grow their professional learning communities.

4. Engage in professional development offered by staff members based on learning opportunities that have been supported by the principal in his/her strategic planning (e.g., professional learning community celebrations, teacher conference presentations).

5. Ask the principal how he/she decides which professional learning communities and/or opportunities are worthy of his/her support.

# MANAGEMENT OF PEOPLE & PROCESS

Observation Notes for Improvement of Learning

**Observation 1**                                                Date: [                    ]

[                                                                                    ]

**Observation 2**                                                Date: [                    ]

[                                                                                    ]

**Observation 3**                                                Date: [                    ]

[                                                                                    ]

**Observation 4**                                                Date: [                    ]

[                                                                                    ]

# Inquiry Cycle Tool: A tool to Assist Principal Supervisors Support Principals as instructional Leaders

**CENTER *for* EDUCATIONAL LEADERSHIP**
university of washington · college of education

Version 2.0

*Source:* © 2014 University of Washington Center for Educational Leadership.

Edited August, 2015.

This publication is provided as part of the training programs of the University of Washington Center for Educational Leadership.
This publication is not sold separately.

# Instructional Leadership **Inquiry Cycle Tool**

**PHASE 1**

**ANALYZE EVIDENCE TO DEVELOP PROBLEMS OF PRACTICE**

Principal and principal supervisor gather and analyze evidence to identify student learning problems and problems of teaching practice. Critical questions in this phase include: *What are the learning strengths and challenges of student learning? What are the related instructional strengths and challenges of teaching practice?*

**PHASE 4**

**ANALYZE IMPACT**

Principal and principal supervisor analyze the results of the instructional leadership inquiry cycle. Critical questions in this phase include: *What was learned about leadership practice and its impact on teacher practice and student learning? What are the implications for the next inquiry cycle?*

**1 ANALYZE EVIDENCE**

**4 ANALYZE IMPACT**

**2 DETERMINE A FOCUS**

**3 IMPLEMENT & SUPPORT**

**PHASE 2**

**DETERMINE AN AREA OF FOCUS**

Principal and principal supervisor analyze evidence to identify a principal instructional leadership area of focus. Critical questions in this phase include: *What type of evidence will be collected to determine the area of focus? What is the principal area of focus for this cycle of inquiry?*

**PHASE 3**

**IMPLEMENT & SUPPORT**

Principal and principal supervisor engage in a series of learning sessions centered on the principal's area of focus. Critical questions in this phase include: *What are the possible actions for a series of learning sessions? How will these sessions improve principal performance?*

# Instructional Leadership **Inquiry Cycle Tool**

## PHASE I: ANALYZE EVIDENCE TO DEVELOP PROBLEMS OF PRACTICE

Principal and principal supervisor gather and analyze evidence to identify student learning problems and problems of teaching practice. Critical questions in this phase include: *What are the learning strengths and challenges of student learning? What are the related instructional strengths and challenges of teaching practice?*

**Steps:**

1. Analyze evidence of student learning to identify a student learning problem.
2. Analyze evidence of instruction to identify a contributing teaching problem of practice.

**CEL Resources:**

- Instructional Leadership Inquiry Cycle Tool
- Creating a Theory of Action for Improving Teaching and Learning

**District Resources:**

- Data gathering tools and processes (e.g., assessment scores, teacher evaluations ratings, walkthrough data)
- School Improvement Plan

## PHASE II: DETERMINE AN AREA OF FOCUS

Principal and principal supervisor analyze evidence to identify a principal instructional leadership area of focus. Critical questions in this phase include: *What type of evidence will be collected to determine the area of focus? What is the principal area of focus for this cycle of inquiry?*

**Steps:**

1. Analyze evidence of principal leadership and determine an area of focus.
2. Generate a theory of action.
3. Determine evidence of success.
4. Determine a date to formally analyze the impact of this inquiry cycle.

**CEL Resources:**

- Instructional Leadership Inquiry Cycle Tool
- Creating a Theory of Action for Improving Teaching and Learning
- Gathering Evidence for 4 Dimensions of Principal Instructional Leadership
- Principal Area of Focus Conversation

**District Resources:**

- School Improvement Plan
- Principal self-assessment
- Principal evaluation and goal setting
- Principal performance data (e.g., climate surveys, 360 evaluations)

## PHASE III: IMPLEMENT AND SUPPORT

Principal and principal supervisor engage in a series of learning sessions centered on the principal's area of focus. Critical questions in this phase include: *What are the possible actions for a series of learning sessions? How will these sessions improve principal performance?*

**Steps:**

1. Co-create a learning plan for principal implementation and principal supervisor support.
2. Implement the learning plan.
   a. Use pre-planning prompts to plan each learning session.
   b. Create a learning agenda for each learning session.
   c. Reflect after each learning session and revise the learning plan if necessary

**CEL Resources:**

- Instructional Leadership Inquiry Cycle Tool
- Walkthrough forms
- Lesson planning templates
- Curriculum guides / grade level standards
- Principal networks
- Videos

## PHASE IV: ANALYZE IMPACT

Principal and principal supervisor analyze the results of the instructional leadership inquiry cycle. Critical questions in this phase include: *What was learned about leadership practice and its impact on teacher practice and student learning? What are the implications for the next inquiry cycle?*

**Steps:**

1. Analyze student and teacher evidence.

2. Analyze principal leadership practice evidence.

3. Prepare written analysis for reflection and feedback.

4. Present cycle to principal supervisor and/or colleagues.

5. Determine whether to continue with same area of focus and inquiry cycle or adjust accordingly.

**CEL Resources:**

- Instructional Leadership Inquiry Cycle Tool
- Analyze Impact Protocol

## PHASE I: ANALYZE EVIDENCE TO DEVELOP PROBLEMS OF PRACTICE

During this phase, the principal and principal supervisor gather and analyze evidence to identify a student learning problem and a teaching problem of practice.

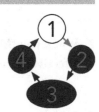

**CEL Resources:**

- Instructional Leadership Inquiry Cycle Tool
- Creating a Theory of Action for Improving Teaching and Learning
- 5 Dimensions of Teaching and Learning

**District Resources:**

- Data gathering tools and processes (e.g. formative and summative assessments, teacher evaluation ratings, observational data, and teacher conversations)
- School Improvement Plan
- System-wide goals and initiatives
- Instructional Framework

## STEP 1: Analyze evidence of student learning to identify a student learning problem.

1. Based on the analysis of data, what are some concerns about student learning?

2. What evidence supports these concerns?

3. What student strengths are there to build upon?

4. What is the specific student learning problem to be addressed in this cycle of inquiry?

5. Why this one over others?

## STEP 2: Analyze evidence of instruction to identify a contributing teaching problem of practice.

1. What would teaching practice look like and sound like if the student learning problem is effectively addressed?

2. When you think about this student learning problem, which teaching practices effectively address it?

3. Which concern you the most?

4. What is the specific problem of teaching practice to be addressed in this cycle of inquiry?

5. Why this one over others?

## PHASE II: DETERMINE AN AREA OF FOCUS

During this phase, the principal and principal supervisor gather and analyze evidence of principal practice to identify a principal instructional leadership area of focus.

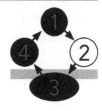

**CEL Resources:**

- Instructional Leadership Inquiry Cycle Tool
- Creating a Theory of Action for Improving Teaching and Learning
- Gathering Evidence for 4 Dimensions of Principal Instructional Leadership
- Principal Area of Focus Conversation Phase II
- 4 Dimensions of Instructional Leadership Framework

**District Resources:**

- School Improvement Plan
- Principal self-assessment
- Principal evaluation and goal setting
- Principal performance data (e.g., climate surveys, 360 evaluations)
- Principal Leadership Framework
- High-priority practices
- System-wide goals and initiatives

### STEP 1: Analyze evidence of principal leadership and determine an instructional leadership area of focus

1. What would a principal be doing if she was effectively addressing the teaching problem of practice and identified student learning problem?

2. When you think about this teaching problem of practice and student learning problem, which leadership practices effectively address it?

3. Which concern you the most?

4. What is the specific problem of principal instructional leadership practice to be addressed in this cycle of inquiry?

5. Why this one over others?

## STEP 2: Generate a theory of action.

Using the responses above, generate a theory of action that explains the specific changes the principal intends to make to improve teaching and learning in the school.

**If the principal . . .**


**then teachers will be able to . . .**


**so that students will be able to . . .**


## STEP 3: Determine evidence of success.

Based on the data and information gathered, what is the current state of student learning, teaching and instructional leadership practice? What is evidence of success and how will the evidence be measured?

| AREA OF CHANGE | PRINCIPAL PRACTICE | TEACHING PRACTICE | STUDENT LEARNING |
|---|---|---|---|
| **What is the current reality?** | | | |
| **What will success look like?** | | | |
| **How will success be measured?** | | | |

## STEP 4: Determine a date to formally analyze the impact of this inquiry cycle.

Determine a date for the close of this inquiry cycle. Consider the area of focus and the principal's learning needs and the schedule established for review of the principal's progress.

**Date:**

---

**PHASE III: IMPLEMENTATION AND SUPPORT**
**During this phase, the principal and principal supervisor engage in action, study and learning around the identified area of focus.**

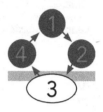

**CEL Resources:**

- Instructional Leadership Inquiry Cycle Tool
- Learning Session Opening Conversation Phase III
- Learning Session Closing Conversation Phase III
- Example Learning Session Opening Conversation with Principal Web

**District Resources:**

- Walkthrough forms
- Lesson planning templates and curriculum guides
- Principal networks
- Videos
- Instructional coaches

## STEP 1: Restate the principal area of focus and co-create the learning plan.

| Learning Plan | Possible Actions: | Why do you think these actions are likely to improve principal performance? |
|---|---|---|
| Learning Session 1<br><br><br>DATE:<br>TIME: | | |
| Learning Session 2<br><br><br>DATE:<br>TIME: | | |
| Learning Session 3<br><br><br>DATE:<br>TIME: | | |
| Learning Session 4<br><br><br>DATE:<br>TIME: | | |

## STEP 2: Implement the Learning Plan.

During this phase, the principal supervisor, with input from the principal, plans and reflects on each individual learning session.

## STEP 2A: Use pre-planning prompts to plan each learning session.

This section is designed to guide the pre-planning process for an individual learning session. Respond to the following questions and incorporate responses into the planning process. You will repeat this process for each learning session that makes up the learning plan.

**PURPOSE:** What is the purpose of the learning session? How does the purpose relate to the ongoing work of the school? The area of focus for the principal? The teachers? The students?

**OUTCOMES:** What are the outcomes for this learning session? What evidence will be collected?

**LEARNING ACTIVITIES:** Which learning activities will best further the principal's learning (e.g., observing classrooms, co-planning, professional development, examining student work)?

**TEACHING/COACHING PRACTICES:** Which teaching/coaching practices will best further the principal's learning (e.g., modeling, coaching and feedback, inquiry)?

**JOINT WORK:** How will the planning of this session ensure that the principal supervisor and principal engage in joint work? That the principal has ownership for the learning? What strategies will be used? Which questions will be posed? How will the opening be used?

**EVIDENCE GATHERING:** How will evidence of the principal's practice be gathered throughout the visit? What will be observed with this principal? How will the information be shared?

**RESOURCES:** What materials will be used in this session? Are there other resources (including people) that need to be deployed? How will you share with the principal? Prior to the visit? During the visit? After the visit?

OTHER CONSIDERATIONS: What needs to be communicated to the principal before the session? How will this be communicated? What does the principal need to prepare? What needs to be communicated to others who might be joining the session?


OTHER:



## STEP 2B: Create the learning agenda for each learning session.

This section is designed to support the crafting of a well-organized learning session. Using the responses above in step 2a, organize and plan each individual learning session.

Date:                    Duration:                    Location:

| CONTENT | PROCESS | TIME AND MATERIALS |
|---------|---------|--------------------|
| **Opening**<br><br>• What is the purpose of the session? What do we want to learn?<br><br>• How will I introduce the purpose for the session?<br><br>• How will I communicate the through-line from improved principal practice to improved teacher practice and student learning — the theory of action for our work together?<br><br>• How will I communicate a "can-do" attitude along with urgency?<br><br>• How will I communicate my commitment to being a co-learner in the process? | | |

| CONTENT | PROCESS | TIME AND MATERIALS |
|---|---|---|
| **Review agreed-upon actions from the last visit**<br><br>• How will I bring forward agreed-upon actions?<br>• How will I address the current status of these actions? | | |
| **Review evidence of success**<br><br>• How will I bring back the evidence of success for this cycle?<br>• How will we note any progress to date?<br>• How will we collect evidence of progress during this session? | | |
| **Engage in the planned activity for the learning session**<br><br>• What do I anticipate the principal will struggle with? How will I mitigate this struggle?<br>• What will I do to foster time for the principal to think, engage, and ask questions during the learning activity?<br>• What questions, statements, and actions will I use to elicit and assess principal understanding?<br>• How will I continually gather evidence of principal practice? | | |

| CONTENT | PROCESS | TIME AND MATERIALS |
|---|---|---|
| **Closing**<br><br>• How will the principal summarize the outcomes for the session?<br>• How will I plan for reflection on the success of the visit?<br>• How will I collect these reflections?<br>• How will I use the reflections to inform the principal's next steps?<br>• What other artifacts will I collect to inform principal planning? | | |

## STEP 2C: Reflect after each learning session and revise the learning plan if necessary.

The principal and principal supervisor respond to the following questions to summarize each learning session. After reflection, both the principal and principal supervisor keep a copy to use as a running record of principal progress over time.

1. **What did we learn today?**

2. **What is the state of the principal's practice in relationship to the area of focus? What growth is being made? What is the evidence?**

3. **What do we need to pay attention to?**

4. **What are the principal's next steps?**

5. **What are the principal supervisor's next steps?**

6. **How will we communicate in-between sessions?**

7. **What do we need to consider in planning the next session on the learning plan? How, if at all, does the next session need to be revised?**

## PHASE IV: ANALYZE IMPACT

During this phase, the principal and principal supervisor analyze and formally close an inquiry cycle. This phase requires a presentation of learning and impact for feedback.

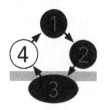

**CEL Resources:**

- Analyze Impact Protocol
- Instructional Leadership Inquiry Cycle Tool

## STEP 1: Analyze student and teacher evidence.

The principal and principal supervisor reflect on the following questions:

1. **What has changed with student learning since the beginning of this cycle? What is the evidence?**

2. **What has changed with teaching practice since the beginning of this cycle? What is the evidence?**

## STEP 2: Analyze principal leadership practice evidence.

The principal and principal supervisor reflect on the following questions:

1. **What has changed with the instructional leadership practice since the beginning of this cycle?**

2. **What is the evidence?**

## STEP 3: Prepare written analysis for reflection and feedback.

In preparation for the presentation of the impact of instructional leadership cycle on teaching practice and student learning, the principal and principal supervisor prepare a written response to the following questions:

1. **What is the specific principal area of focus and theory of action for the inquiry cycle?**

2. **What were the specific learning activities the principal engaged in with the supervisor?**

3. **To what extent did student learning improve in the identified area of need? What is the evidence?**

4. **To what extent did teaching practice improve in the identified area of focus? What is the evidence?**

5. **To what extent did the principal practice improve in the identified area of focus? What is the evidence?**

6. **What promising leadership practices emerged that the principal should continue? What practices should be under consideration for elimination or minimizing?**

7. What ideas have arisen for future leadership cycles of inquiry?

8. What is a focus question that intrigued you during this cycle that the principal supervisor and/or colleagues can provide feedback on?

9. To what extent did the principal supervisor's support impact the outcome of this cycle on principal practice, teaching practice and student learning?

## STEP 4: Present cycle to principal supervisor and/or colleagues.

Use the Analyze Impact Protocol to share results of engaging in the cycle. The presentation allows for the principal and/or principal supervisor to hear and reflect on the feedback in order to make adjustments to future cycles.

## STEP 5: Determine whether to continue with the same area of focus and inquiry cycle or adjust accordingly.

The principal and principal supervisor set a date to develop the next inquiry cycle.

# REFERENCES

Bill & Melinda Gates Foundation. (2014). *Teachers know best: Teachers' views on professional development.* Seattle, WA: Author.

Boaler, J. (2013). Ability and mathematics: The mindset revolution that is reshaping education. *FORUM, 55,* 143–152.

Bransford, J., & Schwartz, D. S. (2008). It takes expertise to make expertise: Some thoughts about why and how and reflections on the themes in chapters 15–18. In K. A. Ericsson (Ed.), *Development of professional expertise: Toward measurement of expert performance and design of optimal learning environments.* New York, NY: Cambridge University Press.

Bryk, A., Gomez, L., Grunow, A., & LeMahieu, P. (2015). *Learning to improve: How America's schools can get better at getting better.* Cambridge, MA: Harvard Education Press.

Cobb, P., Gresalfi, M., & Hodge, L. (2009). An interpretive scheme for analyzing the identities that students develop in mathematics classrooms. *Journal for Research in Mathematics Education, 40*(1), 40–68.

Council of Chief State School Officers (CCSSO). (2015). *Model principal supervisor standards.* Washington, DC: Author.

Dunleavy, T. K. (2015). Delegating mathematical authority as a means to strive toward equity. *Journal of Urban Mathematics Education, 8*(1).

Ericsson, K. A., & Pool, R. (2016). *Peak: Secrets from the new science of expertise.* New York, NY: Houghton Mifflin Harcourt.

Fink, S., & Markholt, A. (2011). *Leading for instructional improvement: How successful leaders develop teaching and learning expertise.* San Francisco, CA: Jossey-Bass.

Gallucci, C., Van Lare, M., Yoon, I., & Boatright, B. (2010). Instructional coaching: Building theory about the role and organizational support for professional learning. *American Educational Research Journal, 47*(4), 919–963.

Hattie, J. (2009). *Visible learning: A synthesis of over 800 meta-analyses relating to achievement.* London, UK: Routledge.

Honig, M. (2012). District central office leadership as teaching: How central office administrators support principals' development as instructional leaders. *Educational Administration Quarterly, 48*(4).

Jerald, C. D. (2012). *Leading for effective teaching: How school systems can support principal success.* Seattle, WA: Bill & Melinda Gates Foundation.

Johnson, S., & Donaldson, M. (2007). Overcoming the obstacles to teacher leadership. *Educational Leadership, 65*(1), 8–13.

Katz, S., & Dack, L. (2013). *Intentional interruptions: Breaking down learning barriers to transform professional practice.* Thousand Oaks, CA: Corwin.

Kazemi, E., & Stipek, D. (2001). Promoting conceptual thinking in four upper elementary mathematics classrooms. *Elementary School Journal, 102,* 59–80.

Kilpatrick, J., Swafford, J., & Findell, B. (Eds.). (2001). *Adding it up: Helping students learn mathematics.* Mathematics Learning Committee, National Resource Council. Washington, DC: National Academy Press.

Learning Forward. (2011). *Standards for professional learning.* Oxford, OH: Author.

Lortie, D. (1975). *Schoolteacher: A sociological study.* Chicago, IL: University of Chicago Press.

Marzano, R. J., Frontier, T., & Livingston, D. (2011). *Effective supervision: Supporting the art and science of teaching.* Alexandria, VA: Association for Supervision and Curriculum Development.

The New Teacher Project. (2015). *The mirage: Confronting the hard truth about our quest for teacher development.* Brooklyn, NY: Author.

Stein, M. K., & Nelson, B. (2003). Leadership content knowledge. *Educational Evaluation and Policy Analysis, 25*(4), 423–448.

Stein, M. K., & Smith, M. S. (2011). *Five practices for orchestrating productive mathematics discussions.* Reston, VA: National Council of Teachers of Mathematics.

Supovitz, J. A., & May, H. (2011). The scope of principal efforts to improve instruction. *Educational Administration Quarterly, 47*(2), 332–352.

University of Washington Center for Educational Leadership (CEL). (2012). *4 dimensions of instructional leadership.* Seattle, WA: Author.

Van de Walle, J. A., Karp, K. S., & Bay-Williams, J. M. (2013). *Elementary and middle school mathematics, teaching developmentally, the professional development edition for mathematics coaches and other teacher leaders.* New York, NY: Pearson.

Yackel, E., & Cobb, P. (1996). Sociomathematical norms, argumentation, and autonomy in mathematics. *Journal for Research in Mathematics Education, 27*(4), 458–477.

# INDEX

90–92; peer, 61; as pre-planning prompt, 159; principal supervisor relationship with, 109–110; teachers and, 18–19; team availability of, 50

Cobb, P., 41

Common Core Standards, 4

Context: affirmation conversation setting of, 100; in next step conversation, 101; PD consideration of, 51–52; planning conversation setting of, 98; for reflection conversation, 103

Continuous learning and improvement culture, 4, 9, 75, 125, 130, 133

Council of Chief State School Officers (CCSSO) Model Principal Supervisor Standards, 109

Curriculum and pedagogy dimension, 33, 35, 38–39

**D**

Dack, L., 4

Data: final math studio use of, 126; 5D use of, 35–36; PD use of, 49; strategic follow-up and, 92

Deploying resources subdimension, 11, 14–17, 25

Discussion prompt chart, 29

Discussion questions: for chapter 1, 8; for chapter 2, 21; for chapter 3, 44; for chapter 4, 62–63; for chapter 5, 83; for chapter 6, 97; for chapter 7, 115

**E**

English language learners (ELLs), 1, 58, 86, 88, 96; math department performance gaps of, 51–52, 65; school-wide focus on, 60, 69; work persistence of, 126

Ericsson, K. A., 5, 6

Evidence, 80, 93, 104; affirmation conversation sharing of, 100; of classroom practice collection of instructional leaders, 32; inquiry cycle tool use of, 151, 156, 161, 163; next step conversation sharing of, 101; pre-planning prompts gathering of, 159; principal supervisor and, 109, 132–133, 135, 139, 143, 146

Expectations for implementation step, 64, 67, 71

**F**

Feedback, 49, 85, 125, 129; affirmation conversation use of, 100; in inquiry cycle tool, 164–165; math department use of, 61; principal supervisor ongoing support by, 110; strategic follow-up cycles of, 88; student independence, 96. *See also* Targeted feedback

s*Five Practices for Orchestrating Productive Mathematics Discussions* (Stein and Smith), 126

5 Dimensions of Teaching and Learning (5D) framework, 36, 42;

assessment for student learning dimension of, 33, 35, 40; classroom environment and culture dimension of, 33, 35; curriculum and pedagogy dimension of, 33, 35; leader expertise building of, 34; organization of, 33; purpose dimension of, 33, 35; research study of, 33; student engagement dimension of, 33, 35

Follow-up. *See* Strategic follow-up

4 Dimensions of Instructional Leadership framework (4D), 4, 9, 19, 49, 132; allocation of resources guiding questions in, 25, 142; CEL creation of, 10; deploying resources subdimension in, 11, 25; high-impact practices of, 10; instructional leaders considerations in, 10–11; instructional leaders questions in, 11–12; instructional leadership beliefs of, 22; instructional practice improvement guiding questions in, 24, 49; learning-focused culture subdimension in, 11, 23; management of systems and processes guiding questions in, 26; marshaling resources subdimension in, 11, 25; observation and analysis subdimension in, 11, 24, 29, 49; professional growth subdimension in, 11, 26; shared vision of effective instructor subdimension in, 11, 24; structures of support subdimension in, 11, 26; support for teacher growth subdimension in, 11, 24, 49; talent management subdimension in, 11, 26; vision and mission community engagement in, 12; vision and mission subdimension and guiding questions in, 11, 23

**G**

Goal setting and implementation walkthrough, 30, 45

**H**

Hattie, John, 2

Honig, Meredith I., 132

**I**

Identify need step, 63, 66, 70

Identify structure and resources for opportunity step, 64, 68, 72

ILDs. *See* Instructional leadership directors

Inquiry cycle tool, 110; chart of, 150; phase I: analyze evidence to develop problems of practice in, 151; phase I: CEL resources in, 151, 153; phase I: critical questions for, 150, 151; phase I: district resources for, 151, 153; phase I: step 1: student learning problem identification and questions in, 154; phase I: step 2: teaching problem of practice identification and questions in, 154; phase I: steps in, 151; phase II: area of focus determination in, 151; phase II: CEL resources in, 151, 155; phase II: critical questions for, 150, 151; phase II: district resources for, 152, 155; phase II: step: 1: principal leadership area of focus determination and questions for, 15; phase II: step 2: theory of action generation in, 156; phase II: step 3: evidence of success determination in, 156; phase II: step 4: inquiry cycle impact determination date in, 157; phase II: steps in, 151; phase III: CEL resources in, 152, 157; phase III: critical questions for, 150, 152; phase III: district resources in, 157; phase III: implement and support in, 152; phase III: step 1: principal area of focus restate and learning plan creation, 158; phase III: step 2: learning plan implementation in, 158; phase III: step 2A: pre-planning prompts use in, 158–160; phase III: step 2B: agreed-upon actions in, 161; phase III: step 2B: closing in, 162; phase III: step 2B: evidence of success review in, 161; phase III: step 2B: learning agenda opening in, 160; phase III: step 2B: planned activity engagement in, 161; phase III: step 2C: learning session reflection and revisal questions for, 162; phase III: steps in, 152; phase IV: analyze impact in, 153; phase IV: CEL resources in, 153, 163; phase IV: critical questions in, 150, 153; phase IV: step 1: student and teacher evidence analysis questions in, 163; phase IV: step 2: principal leadership practice evidence analysis and questions for, 163; phase IV: step 3: reflection and feedback written analysis and questions in, 164–165; phase IV: step 4: cycle presentation in, 165; phase IV: step 5: inquiry cycle area of focus determination or adjustment in, 165; phase IV: steps in, 153

Instructional leaders, 133; content area understanding of, 2–3; continuous improvement culture of, 4, 9, 125; deploying resources by, 14–15; effective instruction shared vision of, 20; 4D considerations of, 10–12, 32; improvement of instructional practice dimension use of, 49; increased accountability of, 106; instructional leadership expertise of, 2; instructional practice improvement questions of, 20–21; management of people and processes questions of, 18; marshaling resources by, 14; observation and analysis use of, 20; professional growth steps of, 17; professional learning leadership roles of, 43; PSF goal and vision of, 107–108, 116–117; reciprocal accountability role of, 6–7, 105; resources marshaling and deploying questions of, 15; school district role in supporting, 105; structure support of, 17; student learning knowledge of, 7; talent management of, 17; teacher growth support of, 20, 50; teacher learning support of, 3, 7, 125; teacher performance improvement focus of, 5; unbiased evidence of classroom practice collection of, 32

Instructional leadership, 131–133; aim of, 9; core beliefs in, 22; focus lack in, 10; instructional leaders expertise in, 2; shared vision in, 9

Instructional leadership directors (ILDs), 121, 131. *See also* Principal supervisor

Instructional practice improvement, 49; core ideas in, 138; document consideration and potential evidence in, 139–140; observation and form for, 140–141; questions in, 20–21, 24, 49, 138–139; student learning impact of, 129

grade classroom observation of, 34–35; strengths and verges examining in, 42–43; student academic discourse focus of, 27–28; student talk guide phrases in, 28, 29; students think and talk like mathematicians goal of, 51; studio classroom structure of, 28; teacher activities engagement in, 30, 31; teacher learning clarity aim in, 42; teacher-created discussion prompt chart in, 29; team notices and wonders about assessment for student learning in, 39–40; team notices and wonders about classroom environment and culture in, 41; team notices and wonders about curriculum and pedagogy in, 38–39; team notices and wonders about purpose in, 37; team notices and wonders about student engagement in, 38

Memorandum of understanding (MOU), 111

MOU. *See* Memorandum of understanding

rationale in, 99; teacher area of focus reflection and rationale in, 98

Planning for Focused Professional Learning, 50, 59; clear teacher and student outcomes step and rationale in, 64; consider content step and rationale in, 63; expectations for implementation step and rationale in, 64; identify need step and rationale in, 63; identify structure and resources for opportunity step and rationale in, 64; questions to ask in, 63–64; support plan step and rationale in, 64

PLCs. *See* Professional learning communities

Pool, R., 5

"Post holing," 3, 6

Pre-planning prompts, learning sessions: evidence gathering as, 159; joint work as, 159; learning activities in, 159; other considerations in, 160; outcomes as, 159; purpose in, 159; resources as, 159; teaching/coaching practices as, 159

Principal, 15, 132, 158, 163; in professional learning session, 73–74, 77; school districts and, 105–108, 112, 131; targeted feedback role of, 94. *See also* Principal Support Framework; Professional learning session sponsorship

Principal supervisor: allocation of resources core ideas for, 142; allocation of resources document consideration for, 143; allocation of resources guiding questions for, 142; allocation of resources observation activities of, 144; allocation of resources observation form of, 144–145; allocation of resources potential evidence for, 143; buffering and brokering of, 111–112; central office support of, 114–115; coaching relationship change and evolvement in, 109–110; collecting and organizing evidence system creation of, 133; conversational architectures modeling of, 110; desired qualifications of, 122; evidence use model of, 132; evidence-gathering methods of, 109; 4D use of, 132; high-priority standards focus of, 109; historical role as, 113; improvement of instructional practice core ideas for, 138; improvement of instructional practice document consideration for, 140; improvement of instructional practice guiding questions for, 138–139; improvement of instructional practice observation activities of, 140; improvement of instructional practice observation form of, 141;

improvement of instructional practice potential evidence for, 139; inquiry cycle tool use of, 110; instructional leadership clear evidence development of, 133; instructional leadership continuous assessment of, 133; key responsibilities of, 121–122; ongoing feedback support of, 110; people and processes management core ideas for, 145–146; people and processes management document consideration for, 147; people and processes management guiding questions for, 146; people and processes management observation activities of, 147; people and processes management observation form of, 148; people and processes management potential evidence for, 146; position summary of, 121; preferred background and work experience of, 122–123; principals' instructional leadership assessment tool of, 131–132; principals' strength and weaknesses familiarity of, 131; questions reflection of, 133–134; role revising of, 109, 113; sample job description for, 121–123; tool criteria amending of, 133; two-way communication of, 111; vision and mission and culture building core

ideas for, 134; vision and mission and culture building document consideration for, 136; vision and mission and culture building guiding questions for, 135; vision and mission and culture building observation activities of, 136; vision and mission and culture building observation form of, 137; vision and mission and culture building potential evidence for, 135

Principal Support Framework (PSF): action area 1: guiding questions in, 116–117; action area 1: principals as instructional leaders goal and vision in, 107–108, 116–117; action area 2: guiding questions in, 117–119; action area 2: system of support for developing principals goal and vision in, 108–109, 117–119; action area 3: guiding questions in, 119–120; action area 3: principals and central office partnership goal and vision in, 112–113, 119–120; CEL development of, 107; central office leaders in, 116; learning at all levels support of, 115

Professional development (PD): clarity lack in, 50; context consideration in, 51–52; implementation expectations in, 59–60; math goal prioritizing and curriculum materials help in, 58; Moriarty and, 13, 73–74, 78–80; need identification in, 53, 58; revision and development in, 62; structure and resources identification in, 61–62; student learning and instructional practice and observation data use in planning for, 49; student talk planning in, 53; students think and talk like mathematicians goal of, 51; support plan articulation in, 60–61; teacher and student outcome clarification in, 58–59; teacher practice low-impact of, 50; types of, 49

Professional growth subdimension, 11, 17, 26

Professional learning communities (PLCs), 17, 49, 79, 80, 90, 146; math department time prioritization in, 61; Mountain View School buffering of, 111–112

Professional learning session: clear principal message in, 74; continuous learning communication in, 75; implementation expectations in, 80; intentional language choice in, 75; leader role in, 74, 83–84; leader understanding and learning alongside teachers in, 77–78; learning and implementation connection in, 82; learning opportunities connection in, 80; math consultant observation in, 78–79;

Moriarty closing of, 81–82; Moriarty opening of, 75–77; principal participation intentional in, 77; principal time use in, 77; principal's sponsorship of, 73; session opening bad example for, 75; sponsorship for implementation in, 74; strategic communication in, 73; student learning vision in, 75; tasks and new textbook use in, 81; teacher and student needs understanding in, 78; teacher learning culture creation in, 78; teacher learning observation in, 79–80; teacher learning specific evidence sharing in, 80; teachers' learning sponsor in, 73–74; vague opening concern in, 75

Professional learning session sponsorship: closing session outline and rationale for, 84; open session outline and rationale for, 83; participation during session outline and rationale for, 84; questions to ask in, 83–84

PSF. *See* Principal Support Framework

Purpose dimension, 33, 35, 39

**R**

Reciprocal accountability, 6–7, 60, 105–106

Reflection conversation: district and school goals review and rationale for, 103; independent and collaborative study next steps in, 104; purpose of, 103; questions and frames for, 103–104; set context and rationale for, 103; student learning evidence and rationale for, 104; targeted feedback cycle commitment in, 104; teacher's area of focus and student learning notice and rationale for, 103